Clock Watchers

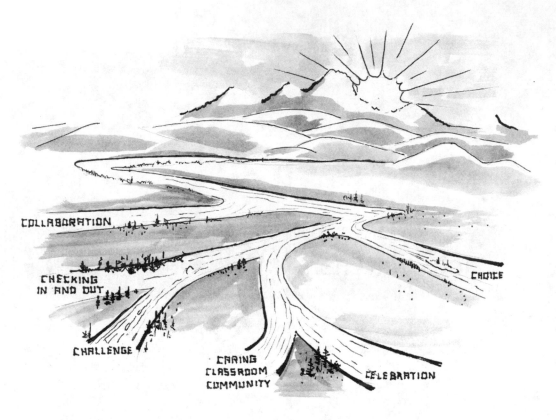

Artwork by Shaun Armour

Clock Watchers

Six Steps to Motivating and Engaging
Disengaged Students Across Content Areas

Stevi Quate

John McDermott

HEINEMANN • PORTSMOUTH, NH

Heinemann
361 Hanover Street
Portsmouth, NH 03801–3912
www.heinemann.com

Offices and agents throughout the world

Library of Congress Cataloging-in-Publication Data
Quate, Stevi.
    Clock watchers : six steps to motivating and engaging disengaged students across content areas / Stevi Quate, John McDermott.
        p. cm.
    Includes bibliographical references and index.
    ISBN-13: 978-0-325-02169-0
    ISBN-10: 0-325-02169-4
  1. Motivation in education—United States. 2. Effective teaching—United States.
3. Learning, Psychology of. I. McDermott, John, 1951 June 22– II. Title.
    LB1065.Q37 2009
    370.15'4—dc22   2009013287

Editor: Lisa Luedeke
Production: Elizabeth Valway
Cover design: Night & Day Design
Composition: Kim Arney
Manufacturing: Steve Bernier

Printed in the United States of America on acid-free paper
13 12 11 10 09 VP 1 2 3 4 5

*To my loving husband, Jim, who always believes in me;
to my grandchildren, who deserve to learn in motivating
and engaging classrooms; and to all my former students,
who taught me about teaching and learning.*

—Stevi

*To my soul mate, Pat, who motivates me
to learn and engages me in life.*

—John

CONTENTS

Acknowledgments ix

Foreword xiii

1 Do We Have Time for Motivation and Engagement? 1
    Stevi's Story 1
    John's Story 3
    Why This Book at This Time? What's the Urgency? 4
    What Does a Teacher Need to Know? 7
    The Six Cs: Creating a Context That Motivates Students and Nurtures Engagement 8
    Why Create a Context That Motivates Students and Nurtures Engagement? 9

2 Caring Classroom Community 12
    A Classroom Snapshot 12
    Emotions and Learning 13
    A Classroom Community 14
    A Step into John and Karen's Classroom 16
    What Happened? 17
    Monitoring Yourself 27
    For More Information 28

3 Checking In and Checking Out 30
    Assessment: Unlived Potential? 31
    How Does Assessment Motivate and Engage? 33
    Pictures of Practice 34
    Plan! Plan! And Plan Some More! 36
    Pre- and Post-assessments 38
    When It Works, When It Doesn't 39
    Tips for Thinking About Pre- and Post-assessments 41
    Ongoing Checking In: Providing Feedback 44
    Assessing Your Assessment Practices 48

4 Choice 49
    Ignite Student Passion 49
    Choice and Motivation 51
    Laying the Foundation 52
    Lesson Examples 57
    Routines and Rituals: Homework 66
    Culture of Choice: Extending Beyond the Classroom 67
    Why Not Offer Choice? 70
    For More Information 71

5 Collaboration **72**
   Introducing Collaboration: Andrea's Story 72
   Why Go Through the Trouble? 75
   Types of Groups 77
   Monitoring the Groups 82
   Designing the Work of the Group 85
   The Class as a Collaborative Community 91
   Putting It All Together 92
   For More Information 94

6 Challenge **95**
   Tina's Story 95
   Challenge and Engagement 96
   In the Zone 98
   George's Story 99
   Why Did Adam Succeed? 101
   Believing in Possibilities 105
   For More Information 106

7 Celebration **107**
   The Poetry Slam 107
   Why Take the Time? 108
   Teacher Stance 111
   Ways to Celebrate 115
   This Is Your Celebration 122

8 Putting It All Together: The Six Cs as a Braided River **123**
   The Evolution of Practice 124
   The Rivers Intertwine 125
   Making Time to Motivate and Engage 136

Appendix **139**

Study Guide **155**

Works Cited **167**

Index **171**

ACKNOWLEDGMENTS

When John and I ran into each other at a conference, little did we know that our casual conversation would lead to a book. In the lobby of the conference hotel, we picked up the threads of conversations that we'd begun years before when we taught together. Once again John argued that motivation was the biggest challenge teachers faced while I shook my head and insisted that it was engagement. From that exchange we started our journey together to discover how students learn deeply and passionately. We studied the research on motivation and engagement, worked in classrooms across our state, and interviewed teachers and students from a variety of settings. To our surprise, that journey finally ended up in this book. We owe a multitude of people our mutual gratitude! In particular, both of us want to send our heartfelt thanks to the following:

- Susan Sparks, for inviting the two of us to the conference that began this journey

- Marjorie Larner, who encouraged us to submit a proposal to Heinemann and introduced us to Leigh Peake

- Lisa Luedeke, our gracious and patient editor, who encouraged us and didn't laugh at our novice mistakes

- All our former students who sat in our classrooms at Meritt Hutton Middle and High, St. Mary's Elementary, MacDonnel Central High, Northglenn Junior High, Thornton High, and Horizon High—your vibrancy and honesty taught us important lessons about honoring your thinking and listening carefully to your ideas

- Teacher candidates whose early teaching we continually learned from: Annie Fisher, Andrea Rodriquez, Olivia Bridges, Dave Carr, Jennifer Rike, and all of the rest of you

- All the administrators and coaches who welcomed us in your schools to think about motivation and engagement, especially Joan Watson, Robert Bishop, Beth Hayes, Beth Lombardi, and Karstin Sutton

- Kathleen Wilson, for believing in us from the get-go and for inviting us to work with teachers in southern Colorado

- More teachers than we can list here: Karen Hartman, Kara Kurtz, Nancy Steinke, Martha McFarland, Shaun Armour, Karen Pacheco, Cindy Calder, David Singer, Marne Gulley, Shereen AsaBueed, Matt Brothers, Pam Newman, Scott Murphy, Noreen Miller, and Katherine Keyes

- Steve Lash and Lou Ann Nelson—you're amazing teachers and it was an honor learning from and with you

Each of us has a long list of people we want to personally acknowledge, a list longer than space will allow. So among many others, John wants to especially thank

- My parents, Joe and Gladys McDermott, who taught me to respect and care for others

- Joe, Ray, Jim, and Margie, who taught me to collaborate

- My daughters, Katie and Maggie, who challenge me to excel

- After thirty-one exhilarating years of marriage, my wife, Pat, for every glorious day together

Stevi would like to add special thanks to

- My higher ed Critical Friends Group, who listened to me, asked questions, and expected this book to make it to press: Sam Bennett, Nancy Shanklin, Deanna Sands, and Heidi Barker

- My friends at PEBC who trusted that this book would tell the story it needed to tell: Annie Patterson, Suzanne Plaut, and Paula Miller

- My dad, Larry Quate, and my mom, Jeanne Trevathan, who encouraged me at every turn; how I wish you two were alive to see our book in print

- Dean and Theresa Kimpel, my spectacular son and his wonderful wife, for support and their lack of surprise that this book was to be

- My marvelous husband, who never complained despite the late dinners because I had one more chapter to finish, the days I spent away from home so I could collect more research, and the constant stories of another teacher who knew how to motivate and engage; Jim, you believed in our work, knew we'd finish this book even when we doubted it, and offered the best support ever at all times—thank you!

And this book couldn't have happened without the inspiration of Connor and Cali. Connor, I thought of you as I watched your well-meaning teachers forget about the importance of engagement, and, Cali, I saw your glow when you knew you were great in math. You showed me how strength builds motivation. Because of you two and John's future grandchildren, we wrote this book with a sense of urgency and immediacy.

FOREWORD

Just other day I caught myself on the verge of muttering words I most detest hearing from colleagues: "These kids aren't motivated—they don't care and I don't know what else to do."

The thoughts were directed at two of my students in particular. The first was Michael, a senior heading to the University of Colorado and the second was PJ, a freshman heading to juvenile hall. All semester, I struggled to motivate and engage both of them. Michael, highly proficient in playing the game of school, had learned how to get the grade without doing much thinking. PJ, highly proficient in avoiding work, had learned how to provoke the teacher to get out of class so he didn't have to think. Although their approaches to school differed, both were playing a dangerous game in which they would surely end up the losers. All semester I desperately tried to figure out how to engage and motivate these two young men.

Thankfully, *Clock Watchers: Six Steps to Motivating and Engaging Disengaged Students* landed on my doorstep soon after. As I read, I couldn't help but think about my own students. I started brainstorming ways I could adapt and tweak activities so they fit into my own curriculum and instruction. The feeling of "There's nothing else I can do," soon vanished.

Inside this easy-to-read book I found a treasure trove of research-based instructional strategies that would prove to have immediate results. Monday morning I began trying some of what I had read over the weekend. Sure enough, I saw results. As a veteran teacher of twenty-five years, I knew the six Cs—caring classroom community, checking in/checking out, challenge, collaboration, choice, and celebration—were instructional principles behind effective teaching. The challenge, however, was fitting in and applying them on a day-to-day basis. But authors Stevi Quate and John McDermott do an extraordinary job explicitly showing the reader what each concept looks like in action. A full chapter is devoted to each of the motivating Cs, neatly laying out what it means and how to implement it in the classroom. Helpful examples of assignments and projects from across content areas, which naturally incorporate and promote these motivators, are described in detail, showing teachers how considering these six concepts in all we do ultimately leads to motivation and engagement. In the final chapter, they discuss weaving all six Cs together.

Schools will always have compliant students willing to sit through poor instruction and silly activities in order to get high marks. However, these students are not the ones who push us to change. The students who really make us earn our dough are the ones who challenge us to think about our effectiveness, who demand authenticity. Our profession *obligates* us to motivate and engage our students. *Clock Watchers* supports teachers who want to create classrooms where real world learning takes place. In our quest to grow 21st century learners, we must constantly search for better ways to connect with our students. Whether your students are players of the game of school or are "social loafers" this book will fortify you through those difficult times when you feel like there's nothing left to try.

So instead of cringing the next time your colleagues utter the words, "These students don't care," hand them this book. Describe your personal struggles and your experience with the six Cs so they know you know what they're going through. Then point out a few of your favorite ideas.

As you walk away, smile, knowing you have made a difference.

—Cris Tovani

Do We Have Time for Motivation and Engagement?

Stevi's Story

Long before I walked into the classroom as a teacher, I was curious about motivation. Perhaps it's because as a high school student, I lacked motivation to do the academic tasks required of me but had a strong motivation to get good grades. Those grades were important, but doing the work wasn't. Even then I found it curious that as an avid reader (Beers 1998), I resisted whatever we were required to read and often resorted to CliffsNotes. Yet I had read books like *Treasure Island*, *1984*, and *Brave New World* on my own. I had my book next to my bed that I read every night and most afternoons when school ended. An assigned novel, though, killed my interest.

It wasn't that way when I was younger. I remember being highly motivated to master cursive when I was the new student in a school where the students had been taught cursive the year before. I was motivated to master addition and pestered my father to give me long sets of numbers to add after I had finished my homework. I was motivated to learn about Nebraska history and devoured Willa Cather novels at an early age. I was motivated to write the short stories my fourth-grade teacher assigned us. I still recall rewriting one line of dialogue over and over so it would ring true. When that fourth-grade teacher praised my dream sequence that ended the story, I glowed with pride. (Years later, this praise made me a kind critic as I read middle and high school writers end their stories with a similar version of "and then I woke up from the dream.") Despite my strong motivation to learn in elementary school, in high school my motivation to learn was almost nil.

Little did I know that my history mirrored the research on motivation. The tendency is for motivation to decrease throughout the years (National Research Council 2004; Hidi and Harackiewicz 2000). The suspected reasons for this phenomenon are numerous. Text messaging and playing video games outshine hitting the books. A job with a paycheck at the end of the week beats a class with a grade at the end of the semester. Checking out the boy in the other room is more enticing than checking out amoebas.

As a young teacher, I knew that I wanted the kind of classroom that rebuked the research. I wanted a classroom where students would be motivated to learn, eager to jump into the books we'd discuss and to write thoughtful texts about interesting ideas. I wanted my students to feel my joy in learning that I had as an elementary student. So once I started teaching, I read everything about motivation I could get my hands on, and from that reading, I learned to drum up anticipatory sets like gangbusters, and I could get an energetic debate going over almost any topic. However, even though I could often get kids to nibble at the edges of the learning, I found it difficult to get students to sustain the interest. Only years later did I realize that motivation wasn't enough.

Motivation was what enticed kids to begin the learning game. Dewey, in the early 1900s, talked about education as "catching" and "holding" students. I could catch them, but I couldn't hold them. This tension of catching and holding students reminded me of my interest in birds. Just as I'm motivated to learn about birds, I'll pick up books at the library and subscribe to *Audubon* magazine. The books catch my interest so that I'm willing to begin the game of getting to know birds. However, just like many of my students, those texts don't hold me. Too often, I have a hard time sustaining my attention, and I'm easily pulled away by other interests.

I didn't quite understand what was happening until I read Csikszentmihalyi's ideas about flow (1990, 1997). Reading his description of that experience of getting lost in the activity at hand and the world disappearing because the activity itself consumes one's attention and energy, I began to understand Dewey's concept of holding students. I recalled my own times when I was in flow and recognized how I was held by the experience. I thought about the magical times I'd spent writing when writing worked. I didn't want to stop, and when I did, I could hardly wait to return to it. I remember times when I was so engrossed in writing a story that I'd be thinking about my characters while driving, only to find that I had passed my exit miles before. Not a good plan for driving, but a great experience for the writer.

Reading has often been like that for me. It's easy to get into the flow and get lost in a book. Like many readers, I had experienced moments when I didn't hear someone call my name because I was lost in the story, or times when the characters became as real as my best friends. I knew flow as a reader and a writer. And I could recall numerous other times during nonschool activities when I was totally engaged in my learning: learning to ski when I was the first on the lifts as the sun was breaking over the mountaintops; training my dog as I attended class after class and worked hours on end watching Micky stop when I stopped and walk by my side on command; gardening as I tilled the soil and forgot about the papers that needed to be graded. Yes, I knew flow and I knew what it was like to be a learner who had been caught and held.

When I reflected on those times when I had entered into the state of flow, I realized that I had moved beyond motivation; motivation to learn to ski got me started but wasn't enough to sustain my interest. Engagement was what sustained me. As I lost track of time, I was consumed with knowing more, and I was having fun. Engagement in the activity held me.

That for me was the missing piece of my teaching. How could I motivate my students, and then what could I do to create the context that would engage them?

John's Story

I grew up in a family of seven: four boys, one girl, and two smart parents. My dad was a steelworker for Jones and Laughlin Steel Corporation, and my mother was a housewife. Neither had completed a college education. They loved each of us deeply, but we knew that love of us as people did not always include love of our behavior. We had choices concerning our careers, but the challenge of higher education was nonnegotiable.

Every night our family collaborated around the dinner table. We debated religion, politics, and family matters but with clear norms concerning our language and treatment of each other. Mom and Dad constantly checked on our progress in the classroom, with our chores, and on our treatment of others. Long before I was an educator, I understood the importance of clear and measurable goals. If we did not meet them, we sat down with our parents and planned for success. My parents celebrated our lives. Our accomplishments were displayed on the icebox (yes, it was the '50s!). When we left home, our parents sent us cards, indicating how proud they were of our professional work and reminding us to treat our colleagues and family with love and respect. My parents knew how to motivate and engage their children in learning for life. Long before I read the research about motivation and engagement, I knew it because I had lived it.

School didn't operate in the same way, though. I attended an elementary school in Aliquippa, Pennsylvania. As we sat in our desks on any given morning, an announcement would come on the intercom: "Boys and girls, you are about to hear what happens to students in this school who break the rules. The following rule has been broken." Many mornings we heard the specifics of an offense—tardiness, sassiness, laziness. We knew what was coming next: "Come here, young man." Then we would hear the whack, whack of a paddle meeting the backside of the offender. Cries of pain followed. Yet students continued to break rules and to fight in the halls. More paddling followed. Nothing changed. At an early age, I realized that threats and public punishment shaped the climate of the school but didn't promote excitement in learning.

In this same school, I learned the demoralization of tracking: we had the A class, the B class, and the C class of learners. The difference in how these students were treated was palpable and immoral. You could see it in the faces of the C group; they were sad and bored. Some of these low-tracked learners were motivated to break the rules or act out in anger towards the students from the A group. The A students knew at an early age they were bound for college; the C students knew at an early age they would be working in the steel mill. And years later, on reflecting back to these days, I recognized that most students do rise to the expectations of their teachers.

The lessons from these early years have stayed with me for the entire three decades that I have been in education. I remember hearing the tears of an offender over the intercom and then going home to a family dinner during which we discussed being kind to others. The contrast didn't escape me. In my teaching, I knew I would bring my parents' principles to the classroom, not the principles I learned at school. My parents didn't coerce me into learning; instead, they motivated me through love and high expectations, and they ensured I was engaged through invigorating conversations each night of my young life.

And that's what this book is about. It's about motivation and engagement and ways that we can create the contexts in our schools to heighten both motivation to catch students and engagement to hold them.

Why This Book at This Time? What's the Urgency?

As we work in schools, we see nearly every day why a book on this topic is urgently needed. Along with working as a consultant in various schools across Colorado, each of us is a site professor at two different large urban high schools in the Denver area. As site professors, we mentor teacher candidates and collaborate with practicing teachers and administrators. The schools we work in, along with schools across the nation, face tremendous pressures for teachers to ensure students perform at unprecedented levels.

Because of No Child Left Behind (NCLB), teachers feel the power of the state assessment in shaping their instruction and their professional development, and even if NCLB were to disappear, our hunch is that the pressure to perform would remain. At both of our schools, we watch each year begin with teachers studying data from the previous year's state assessment. Even though administrators build in time for celebrations of growth, teachers focus on the dreary results. Remember, these are urban schools, and they're typical of schools with similar demographics. Often more than twenty percentage points below the state's average proficiency level, the results let teachers know the game they'll play again this year: raise test scores.

School leaders, instructional coaches, district curriculum specialists, and staff developers work long hours determining what teachers need to know in order to close what the newspapers label as the achievement gap. We have seen those solutions run the gamut, some great solutions and some highly questionable: eleven-sentence paragraphs to improve writing scores, a skill-and-drill program hated by both teachers and students as the mandated reading intervention program, standards-based education with the daily objective posted in each classroom, the take-five strategy for solving problems in math, professional learning communities with essential learnings and common assessments, learning walks to monitor teachers' implementation of specific practices, guided reading in all English classrooms at the expense of literature study, sustained silent reading throughout the building, and school uniforms. We've watched the upside and the downside of each of these efforts, and the common variable that we've seen often ignored is captured by the ubiquitous laments of teachers: How do I get the kids to care about their learning? How can I get them to do the work? How can I get them to come to class on time and to bring their books and paper and pens and agenda and homework? In other words, how can teachers motivate and engage their students? Rarely have we seen a school address these concerns, and rarely have we worked with a school where these concerns weren't present.

Ironically, in light of the pressure of NCLB, the issue of motivation and engagement is one that must be addressed. And here's the catch-22:

> When teachers are stressed, they tend to be controlling and demanding with students, and they tend not to provide support and enthusiasm for the students. This has been shown to have a strongly negative effect on the students' motivation and performance. Students need an accepting, supportive, and nourishing context in which to learn, and teachers who are feeling negative emotions and are

not effective in managing them will not be able to supply the needed support to students. Teachers' enthusiasm about teaching has been shown to positively affect students' enthusiasm about learning. (Deci 2006)

Even if NCLB were to disappear, motivation and engagement are so deeply intertwined with substantive learning (Melzer and Hamman 2004) that we see a focus on motivation and engagement as an ethical imperative. Without a sharp focus on motivation and engagement, schools are unlikely to produce students who grow intellectually (NCREL 2005; Guthrie, Wigfield, and Perencevich 2004). A few years ago the National Research Council studied engagement in high schools. The impressive study begins with this statement:

> Learning and succeeding in school requires active engagement—whether students are rich or poor, black, brown, or white. The core principles that underlie engagement are applicable to all students—whether they are in urban, suburban, or rural communities. (2004, 1)

The research shows that motivation and engagement matter in all contexts but in different ways. Students who live in poverty and attend schools where motivation and engagement are missing often leave school at an early age. The dropout rates are stunningly high. In contrast, students from more economically privileged settings can coast by even if they aren't engaged in their studies. Those students may learn less than their more engaged classmates, but they are likely to be given second chances and to graduate (National Research Council 2004). If graduating from high school matters, then motivation and engagement matter (Gewertz 2006), and if deep learning matters, then again motivation and engagement must move to the forefront of education conversations and actions.

When teachers talk about motivation and engagement, the anecdotal stories are often alarming:

"If I can't get a student to come to class, how can I get him to care?"

"You don't know our students."

"They simply don't care about their work and you can't get them motivated, no matter what."

And when researchers study high school students about their level of engagement, the results mirror these anecdotes. In 2004 and 2005, the *High School Survey of Student Engagement* (2005) was given to nearly 171,000 students in twenty-six states. Less than half the students said they did work that made them curious about learning, and less than a third were excited by their classes. If working hard is one element of engagement, then those students were far from engaged. More than half stated that they spent four or fewer hours a week on homework. Yet two-thirds of the students were earning mostly As and Bs.

This is not a recent phenomenon. In the mid-1980s, John Goodlad's (1984) classic study on high schools noted the large number of students who were staring out windows. In the early '90s, LeCompte and Dworkin (1991) were writing about students who were literal school dropouts and those who were still in school but who had "tuned out." Smith and Wilhelm's (2002) landmark research on boys and literacy also highlighted the boredom and disengagement that many of our male students feel. School literacy, for example, just doesn't connect. As poet Jimmy Santiago Baca said in an interview with Bill Moyers, "Reading don't fix no Chevys" (hence the title of the Smith and Wilhelm's book). Without recognizing how school is relevant to their lives, students aren't willing to be caught, let alone held.

What Does a Teacher Need to Know?

If you were to take a peek at the books that line the shelves of our bookcases, you would find a slew of books on motivation and engagement. Stevi might show you a cute flip book that lists activity after activity. John, on the other hand, might pull off his shelf one of several books that promise to give the teacher twenty-five or fifty or even one hundred activities *guaranteed* to motivate. Both of us can tell you stories of presentations we've gone to where presenters listed one tip or trick after another. But tips and tricks are not adequate for meaningful learning, and some that we've heard are just plain silly. Dressing as a historical character might work for teachers with flamboyant personalities, but this trick by itself won't produce the kind of learning that our students deserve. Even though they contain practical ideas that teachers love, these books and presentations simply aren't sufficient to help teachers consider and apply the research on motivation and engagement.

Our book suggests activities that we've seen work in classrooms, but all of the activities are grounded in a framework that is informed by research. This framework, which we call *the six* Cs, is what makes an instructional activity transcend the "tips and tricks" label. Each suggestion has the potential to shape the culture of the classroom, which teachers must intentionally nurture. Our framework provides a way of thinking that will guide planning, teaching, and reflecting on instruction and learning. This framework builds a classroom culture that is likely to produce student motivation and engagement that will result in learning.

Our framework emerges from the research on the psychology of motivation and engagement. Much of this research explores the mind of the student who wants to learn and who persists in doing difficult tasks. This research reminds us that motivated and engaged learners are curious, need to feel competent, and must be convinced that they are in control (Guthrie and Wigfield 1997; Smith and Wilhelm 2006; Deci 2006).

The Six Cs: Creating a Context That Motivates Students and Nurtures Engagement

▶ 1. Caring Classroom Community

Middle schools are often depicted as places where the affective needs of the individual are more important than the academic needs. In contrast, high schools are often portrayed as large impersonal institutions (Goodlad 1984). However, the development of a nurturing classroom community in which students are known well by both the teacher and their classmates matters, whatever their age or grade level. For a teacher to be a "warm demander" (Gay 2000), she must intentionally build the culture of a classroom where students know they're cared for and where they will be supported.

▶ 2. Checking In and Checking Out

Assessment is a hot topic in educational circles, but often the power of assessment isn't realized. One teacher told us, "I can build those pretty charts from the data I've collected, but it won't change a thing for my students." We argue that assessment works better as a verb—as an action—rather than a noun. We've watched how teachers who earnestly check in with their students, provide feedback along the learning journey, and ensure that students are an active part of the check-in–checkout process motivate and engage.

▶ 3. Choice

One of the ways to put students in control of their learning—to build their sense of autonomy—is to ensure that they have voice in their learning. However, choice must be scaffolded and intentional.

▶ 4. Collaboration

Just as motivation theory informs us, relationships matter (Smith and Wilhelm 2006; Gewertz 2006). Students tend to be more motivated and are more likely to be engaged in their learning when they work within a supportive, collaborative context. Students need to know what an effective learning community is and what is not effective.

▶ 5. Challenge

In Colorado, as elsewhere, the three Rs—*rigor*, *relationship*, and *relevance*—have become an educational mantra. We worry, though, about the use of rigor. We've seen rigor defined as tougher standards, increased homework, and reduced student support, and the results have been questionable. Yet we know the power of challenge; when designed appropriately, it is a motivator and an essential factor in engagement. We also know what happens when students aren't challenged appropriately: boredom or even apathy (Csikszentmihalyi 1990).

▶ 6. Celebration

We need to celebrate moments of success, both academically as well as personally. Celebrations can come in many forms, from an end-of-unit coffeehouse event, to a whole-school assembly, to a note sent home to parents. These celebrations set students up for future successes.

Our framework sounds nice and tidy, but we know it's messy. Each strand of our framework is highly interwoven with the others. Just as in a spider's web, one weak strand affects the entire web. No one strand can be ignored, and yet all of them must be strengthened to create that classroom where students are caught and held.

Why Create a Context That Motivates Students and Nurtures Engagement?

▶ To Nurture Curiosity

Psychological studies didn't need to inform us that curiosity influences motivation. Common sense tells us this. Anytime we're curious about something, our interest is high, and we feel motivated to explore and learn. Motivational researchers talk about interest through two constructs: *individual interest* and *situational interest*. Individual interest describes a person's unique interest in a topic, an interest not necessarily connected to school. Situational interest refers to the role of the context in shaping a person's interest. When Stevi's son, Dean, was young, for instance, he was fascinated by butterflies and spent many a summer day with his butterfly net in hand and identification manuals nearby. His individual interest had nothing to do with the classroom; instead, it was personal and might have been influenced by his grandfather, an entomologist. Dean's interest was spurred by his own curiosity and fueled by his growing knowledge. The more he knew, the more he wanted to know.

On the other hand, when Dean was in high school, he had a teacher who loved philosophy, and through masterful teaching, he stirred up the students so that they too were curious about philosophical issues and dilemmas. Because of this situational interest, where the teacher created the context that inspired curiosity, Dean pursued further studies in philosophy when he was in college.

The construct of situational interest provides hope that teachers can do something intentional to catch kids and then to hold them. We don't have to rely on students entering our class already interested in our content, and we can build our repertoire with strategies for tickling their interest. Of course, no teacher wants to bore students; instead, teachers want to nurture imagination, thrill the intellect, and move students to want more, just like Dean's philosophy teacher did. Teachers can build from a student's individual interest, but in the secondary school a focus on situational interest can be highly robust.

The impact of situational interest on motivation is exemplified in research by John Guthrie and Alan Wigfield (1997). They describe a remarkable teacher's kindling of interest by taking students to a hillside outside of school. There students observed insects and formed inquiry questions. After arousing student curiosity, the teacher nurtured their engagement in a rigorous study of insects by building from their questions and showing them how to conduct research that led to answers to their questions. This instructional design was intended to grow literate scientists.

Guthrie and Wigfield's research has informed the work of others. For instance, Perencevich and Taboado (2007), who have worked closely with Guthrie and Wigfield, show how "curiosity charts" motivate. The inquiry process as a way to engage students is detailed in Smith and Wilhelm's book *Going with the Flow* (2006).

One of our major contentions is that creating the context that will motivate students and nurture engagement is not only doable but critical. The way a teacher orchestrates her instruction can tease students into caring and can then build the pathway for sustaining interest. Our six Cs, when braided together, form that context.

▶ *To Respect Students' Need for Competency and Control*

As a teacher thinks about motivation and engagement, it's important to continue peeking into the heads of his students by noting what research tells us about the concept of competency. Remember: the more we know about students' mental and emotional workings, the wiser we can be about our instructional decisions.

In his studies of what makes people happy with their lives, Csikszentmihalyi (1990, 1997) argues that people enter into a state of flow when they are confident that they have the requisite skills necessary to be competent in a given task. Near Stevi is a skateboard park where she's watched young people skate up unbelievable angles for hours on end. She's seen the young men (with an occasional female here and there) fall, scrape elbows, rip the skin off knees, and continue to do it again. One time she asked one of the skateboarders why. His answer: "Because I know I can do it." This skateboarder, like others engaged in challenges, had a strong sense of efficacy, convinced that he would eventually be successful. He was in control and worked hours on end to achieve a goal that he was certain he would attain. In contrast, Stevi asked her nephew why he didn't spend time at the skateboarding park. Randy's answer was simple: "I could never do that!"—and he didn't try. If students doubt their competency, they lose interest, divert attention from their limitations, or flee (Smith and Wilhelm 2006).

The question is: What can teachers do to support the need to feel competent? It's not a gift they can endow on students, but we argue that teachers can create a context that builds the sense of competence. Our framework develops from these notions of competency and control. We're honoring the need of students to feel competent, be autonomous, and be connected to others with similar values. Our focus is on what the teacher can do to nurture this sense of competence and control. It's about a way of thinking to build the kind of classroom that both teachers and students (and administrators and parents) want.

Of course, we're not talking about a silver bullet or about a quick fix. We're talking about building an intentional culture in a classroom and ideally in a school. To build and nurture such a culture takes time. The adolescent who walks into the middle or high school has had years of experiences that have led her to believe that she is or is not capable, that she is cared for or not by the adults in a building, and that she is or is not able to exert control over her academic journey. To change perceptions takes time, and to incorporate all pieces of the framework takes time for teachers.

As Fullan (1993) says, change is a journey, not a blueprint nor a destination. We see that changing the culture of a classroom and of a school is an important journey and one we hope schools will embark on.

Caring Classroom Community

The quality of life improves immensely when there is at least one other person who is willing to listen to our troubles, and to support us emotionally.

—MIHALY CSIKSZENTMIHALYI, *FINDING FLOW: THE PSYCHOLOGY OF ENGAGEMENT WITH EVERYDAY LIFE*

Class is the place where you don't feel left out because everyone knows who you are.

—SARAH, 10TH GRADE, AMERICAN STUDIES PROGRAM

A Classroom Snapshot

It started out as a typical late winter day. Most of the students in the eighth-grade class were sitting obediently, trying to follow the teacher's lecture. The anger in a fellow student's voice jolted John out of the daydream he was slipping into.

"You never get my name right."

"Sit down, please, and don't raise your voice to me," the teacher demanded.

"I have been in this class for six months now, and you still don't know my name."

"Sit down now and apologize for this outburst or you will end up in the principal's office."

"Don't worry, I'm leaving."

As he slammed the door behind him, several students laughed nervously at this outburst. And so did the teacher.

When he returned to class a few days later, the student was humbled and distant. Quietly, he sat in class, often with eyes looking at his desk and tight-lipped. Rarely did he talk to anyone, and rarely did he participate in class.

This memory still seems fresh to John even though it took place decades ago when he was in eighth grade. Unfortunately, John's story is not unique. Stories abound about classrooms that are unfriendly environments. We have heard stories of students being ridiculed and booted out of class for not having a pencil, about teachers posting signs above their doors warning students of dire consequences if they don't study hard enough, and of teachers who publicly humiliate their students. Sadly, these hostile environments have a direct impact on students' willingness to be motivated, let alone to be engaged in their learning (National Research Council 2004). If students perceive an environment to be unsafe, they may shut down emotionally and intellectually. Since we are social creatures who live within the communal realm of schools, teachers must attend to the emotional and social nature of learning throughout the year, particularly as we create a context for motivation and engagement.

Emotions and Learning

There's no question that the pressures teachers face today are tremendous. When John was a young student, there were no state assessments, federal acts like No Child Left Behind, nor public accountability systems with results printed in the newspapers. Today's teachers know that their students' test scores will be scrutinized. Faculty meeting after faculty meeting is dedicated to learning about the test and figuring out ways to change what feels so unalterable: the scores on that test. No wonder teachers assert that they don't have time to do those touchy-feely things such as building a classroom community.

Unfortunately, to ignore the importance of building community is shortsighted. Academic success for many students is interwoven with their emotional perceptions of a classroom (Goleman 1995; Shernoff, Csikszentmihalyi, and Schneider 2003). Does the class feel safe? Are students protected from humiliation? Can they ask a "stupid" question? Is there anyone who knows them well and who cares about how they're doing? These questions tumble around in students' minds from the second they walk into the classroom to the time when they leave at the end of the term. And data shows that a negative response to those questions affects not only student engagement but also the results of that big test at the end of the school year (Elias et al. 2002).

In 1995, Daniel Goleman published his book *Emotional Intelligence*. Many teachers nodded in recognition. They knew how intertwined emotions and learning are. In fact, Goleman argued that emotions rule:

> To the degree that our emotions get in the way of or enhance our ability to think and plan, to pursue training for a distant goal, to solve problems and the like, they define the limits of our capacity to use our innate mental abilities, and so determine how we do in life. And to the degree to which we are motivated by feelings of enthusiasm and pleasure in what we do—or even by an optimal degree of anxiety—they propel us to accomplishment. (89)

Goleman's research suggests that too often educators work from a false dichotomy when they split their activities into affective and academic categories. Because of the interwoven nature of emotions and learning, teachers would be wise to see the affective and academic as braided. Content knowledge is heightened by textures of the affective domain. A way to begin is to acknowledge the role of emotions as a prerequisite to creating a caring classroom community.

This requires that teachers care for the student as an individual as well as a learner. The person and his performance both matter (Gay 2000). Because of the centrality of emotions, if students feel as though the teacher doesn't like them, they often resist the role of learner. In contrast, those students who perceive that their teachers care about them as individuals are more likely to engage and are more likely to worry about letting the teacher down.

A Classroom Community

This message about caring for the person and the student became clear as Stevi watched Annie Fisher learn to teach. Annie was a teacher candidate working on her teaching license in English. For most of the first semester, Annie had been in the school only one day a week, but during the last quarter, she was full-time into her student teaching. Even though she knew the students' names and a little bit about their backgrounds, she wanted to make sure that she knew them well and that they knew each other. One simple routine that began each class period was the unique way she took roll.

"Today I don't want you to say 'here' when I call your name," she explained the first day. "Instead, I want you to answer 'hamburger' or 'pizza,' based on which one you like better." The tenth graders laughed but played along with her. The next day she asked them to name their favorite musicians. On other days, she learned about their birthplaces, their pets, and even their favorite books.

Other activities included having students write their literacy histories. She wanted them to explain when they had learned to read and what had challenged them as they became readers. She had students write personal slogans and posted them around the room. The literary histories were displayed next to the slogans. The room reflected the students who were being educated in that room, and the students knew that Annie cared. At the end of the school year, Stevi interviewed the students about Annie's performance. "Miss," one student stated, "she really cared about us. She made us get to know each other! You know what she did when she took roll each day?"

▶ *Becoming a "Warm Demander"*

But Annie made sure that her students also knew that she cared about their performance. As Geneva Gay argues, care for the person without insistence on performance is "academic neglect" (2000, 48). Annie became a "warm demander" (Gay 2000) who cared enough not to let any student slack. "She made us do the work, Miss. If it wasn't good the first time, she showed us how to make it better and then made us do it," her student explained.

Stevi saw a teacher as a warm demander in another school. This school, too, was filled with students of poverty, and many were immigrants from Mexico or other Latin American countries. Sharon believed in her students' ability to perform well. When she addressed them, she called them scholars, and when they misbehaved, she looked askance as she asked, "And where did the brilliant scholar from yesterday go?"

At the start of the school year, Sharon shared with the students their scores on the state assessment. The majority of the students were in the unsatisfactory or partially proficient ranges. Sharon shared the information with great love, concern, and urgency. After the students learned their scores, Sharon said with sincerity, "Of course you're behind. Just think of how many schools you've been in. You had to miss out on important learning. And some of you are new to English. Of course you're behind because you haven't been speaking English all your lives. But listen to me, carefully. My job is to get you caught up, and that's what we're going to do. You are young scholars, and I'm going to make sure you succeed."

And that's what happened. When the test results came in, those students had made an average of two years' growth on the assessment.

When the students learned that Sharon would not be returning, many were visibly sad. One girl wrote Sharon a note that said, "Thank you for caring enough to believe in me. No teacher has ever done that before."

▶ *Creating the Literacy Club Mind-Set*

Teachers, of course, need to get to know their students well and care enough to demand the best from them. Furthermore, the classroom needs to be a *community* of learners rather than a collection of individuals bound together by a common schedule. Years ago Frank Smith (1987) wrote about the importance of learners knowing that they are part of the "literacy club." Like any club, members of the classroom know that they belong and are welcomed and needed members of the group. Together, members share a common purpose, participate in routines and rituals unique to this group, and follow norms of behavior. Annie's roll-taking procedure, for instance, was a routine and ritual unique to her classroom, and students knew that they belonged.

Within this communal setting, students build an allegiance to their teachers as well as to their classmates that nurtures motivation and engagement. Let's see how this might happen by stepping into John's classroom.

A Step into John and Karen's Classroom

Karen Pacheco and John co-taught Great Books and Great Ideas, a course that prepared juniors and seniors for the Advanced Placement literature and language exams. Endorsing the concept of a caring classroom, the school's curriculum committee dropped the AP label from the class in order to open the door to all students regardless of their grade point average or prior classroom achievements. Brandon arrived on the first day, listened to opening introductions, participated in community-building activities, and investigated the course's challenging assignments. After class, he approached Karen and John.

"I have to drop this class. I'm just a football player. I've never gotten a good grade in any English class and I know this is gonna be way too hard for someone like me."

Much to Brandon's chagrin, Karen and John explained that they had never signed a drop slip for any student. "You will be safe here," they asserted. "It is our job to make sure you learn the material. You will have ample opportunities to succeed." Yes, they continued, he might need to rewrite his essays, but they'd give him feedback. Yes, he would participate in seminars, and they guaranteed that others would listen respectfully to his ideas. Yes, he would do the reading and get constant help with it. Yes, he would stay in the class. And, yes, he would succeed.

When the course ended, Brandon wrote them a thank-you note that moved them close to tears. Among other kind thoughts, he wrote that it was the first time he had actually read and understood classroom assignments. Because of this course, he now planned to go to college. His confidence had grown, and he knew he would succeed.

What Happened?

Like other learners, Brandon had a tremendous fear of failure. Since he had experienced failure in other English classes, Karen and John knew their first task was to create a classroom community steeped in hope and care and yet maintain high expectations for all the students, including struggling learners like Brandon, English language learners, and special education students. They took Geneva Gay's (2000) advice seriously that teachers needed to be warm demanders. But first they had to show the warmth and had to create a community of learners.

▶ *Creating a Community of Learners* Throughout *the School Year*

From the first moment students walked into the classroom, Karen and John greeted them graciously as if they were guests in their homes. Shaking hands and welcoming the students to their room, they began the process of learning each student's name. Because it was a team-taught class, their class load was large—fifty-five students. But they took that as a challenge and learned all the names within the first week of school. At the same time, they made sure students knew each other. When John announced that they would learn the names of each of their classmates, he explained the reasoning for this requirement by telling the story of his teacher who did not know her student's name. In every class activity, Karen and John insisted that students address each other by name, a simple but powerful strategy.

Knowing names opens the door to knowing students, but teachers must also know students' academic history, living situations, hobbies, and learning styles in order to create an optimal learning environment. Students need to be heard and recognized as individuals. With the goal of getting to know their students well, they had students take interest surveys, write about their past histories as learners, and share information not only with their teachers but also with each other. Each activity that started the year was developed with the goals of learning who the members of their class were and of connecting the learners to each other.

Even though this is not an uncommon practice, we have noted that many teachers begin the year with community-building activities but quickly move on to the "real business" of learning and teaching. From our observations of exemplary teachers and classrooms, we have learned that teachers who motivate and engage take time to strengthen classroom relationships *throughout* the school year. Building the caring classroom community is a process, not a lesson plan or two at the start of a term. After all, when midterm grades are due, activities from the first week of school are a distant memory, and often new students have joined the class since those early days.

As a reminder to themselves and their students, Karen and John created charts with student names and parent contact information. On these charts, they noted when they sent postcards home about student successes, met with parents, and contacted them through email. They recorded the times they met with students during lunch and after school. These records ensured that they were contacting all students and not unintentionally overlooking anyone.

▶ Holding High Expectations

A community is bound together for specific reasons. Within a school, that reason is grounded in learning for all. Karen and John knew that they owed it to students to explain that their expectations were high and would remain high for all the individuals in the room. Their expectations mirrored what the National Research Council reported about expectations: "One way that students judge how much teachers care is by whether they hold them to high expectations and make an effort to ensure they are learning" (2004, 54).

Karen and John explained often to students that they were emphasizing learning over grades. They warned that students would be challenged, but challenge would be balanced with hope, and they even offered a "money-back" guarantee: "If you come to class and try to succeed, we will provide the proper scaffolding for your success. If you do not come to class, we will find you at the gas station, cafeteria, your home, sporting events, and we will insist on your attention to the learning." Many students laughed but quickly realized the serious nature of their mission.

Furthermore, Karen and John stressed that as a community, they had responsibilities for each other. No one in that community was to be ignored or deserted. Since they would be a community of learners and teachers, Karen and John shared some of the research that guided their teaching. They understood

Doyle's research (1983) indicating that students need to know *why* they are involved in instructional strategies, not just how to complete the tasks.

During those first few weeks of school, students not only learned names and backgrounds of their classmates but also delved into the challenges and complexities of dealing with difficult relationships and of building an authentic community of learners. John and Karen taught the students about Daniel Goleman's research on emotional intelligence. For several days, they explored the concepts of managing emotions, motivating oneself, recognizing emotions in others, and handling relationships.

▶ *Honoring Multiple Intelligences: The Choice Assignment*

Karen and John designed other assignments during the first quarter to support students in learning the content *and* developing empathy for their classmates. One such assignment followed a discussion of Howard Gardner's research on multiple intelligences. This particular unit focused on two essential questions: What is intelligence? and How is intelligence measured? These questions set the stage for thinking about whom society honors as smart. To illustrate how learning can take many shapes, John and Karen created a choice assignment for one of the readings. They required students to represent their learning through any of the multiple intelligences and then to present their work to a small group (see Chart 2–1). The presentations were quite successful as students marveled at the creativity of their peers, especially those students not known to be academic stars. To debrief the experience, John and Karen returned to the essential question: What is intelligence?

Through exploring their own intelligences, reading some of Gardner's research, and reflecting on the quality of the work of their peers, students understood that intelligence manifests itself in many ways, including through music, sports, art, leadership, literacy, and math. The students reflected on how school typically honors math and literacy but overlooks other areas. This experience set the stage for the year as students learned respect for the different intelligences in the group; empathy grew.

▶ *Encouraging Risk Taking: The Challenge Project*

Right from the start, Karen and John encouraged their learners to take risks with their learning. When they shared the research on self-efficacy, they showed the connection between challenging learning and engagement. To stress the importance of taking meaningful risks in the learning process, one of Karen and John's major assignments required each learner to take an educational, physical, or

Multiple Intelligences	Choices
Intrapersonal	• Write a journal entry from the viewpoint of the main character. • Create a T-chart showing the similarities and differences between you and the main character.
Interpersonal	• Organize a seminar among you and at least three others in class about the reading. Submit a reflection on the seminar, including how your thinking changed as a result of the discussion. • Give a speech to the class from the point of view of the antagonist, telling the serious flaws of the protagonist.
Musical	• Create a song that reflects the theme. • Music selection: find songs that portray the main message of the reading.
Spatial	• Create a drawing, painting, or sculpture representing the reading. • Bring in examples of paintings, drawings, or sculptures that best represent this reading.
Bodily-Kinesthetic	• Perform an interpretive dance based on the reading. • Perform a mime for the class based on the reading.
Mathematical-Logical	• Design a multistep equation representing the complex relationship between the main character and the setting. • Represent the reading through a thorough task analysis of the events in the reading.
Linguistic	• Write a poem representing the reading. • Write an essay concerning the main character's conflict from the point of view of his parents.

Chart 2–1 *Multiple Intelligences*

May be copied for classroom use. © 2009 by John McDermott and Stevi Quate, from Clock Watchers *(Heinemann: Portsmouth, NH).*

emotional risk (Neihart 1999). Of course, these risks had to fall within school safety parameters and had to be legal. The risks had to take students outside their comfort zones. Stressing the importance of braiding together emotions and academics, they explained the academic side of the assignment: to examine the human experience (see Chart 2–2). This was an assignment required of all, including Karen and John. Understanding the importance of modeling, Karen promised to participate in a horseback riding competition while John agreed to work on an article for publication.

When students presented their challenge projects to the class and participated in the seminar, they deepened their sense of community as they learned more about each other and celebrated the small and large risks their classmates had taken. For instance, a football player told about the chess team's surprise when he showed up for the first meeting. The class cheered as a member of the track team successfully completed his first marathon. A young man made the class laugh as he told stories about taking care of his six-month-old sister for two weeks. He changed diapers, fed the baby, and got up at night when she cried. In this community of learners, stories, humor, and shared experiences forged a bond unique to this group.

▌ Reinforcing the Bond: Mind Maps

Assignments throughout the year required students to share their work with the class community and reinforced the message that student work shaped the learning of peers regardless of individual differences. For instance, Karen and John frequently assigned mind maps that required learners to set learning goals and represent their current understanding of course concepts. Mind maps are nonlinear, graphic ways of capturing thinking on a topic. Typically mind maps are created around a word or concept that is placed in the center of the map. Then in a weblike structure, students arrange new ideas, showing how those ideas connect to others. Used for a variety of purposes from brainstorming to note taking to representing a sophisticated understanding of a concept, mind maps can be a creative process for illustrating one's thinking process.

John and Karen introduced the assignment by explaining its purpose: "Mind maps reflect the way your brain organizes information. This process provides you an opportunity to be metacognitive: to think about your thinking. You do not have to be an artist to complete this assignment; we want you to think about how your brain stores information. We'll show you examples of student work and review the rubric. You'll have class time today to work on it, but the remainder of the work will be completed on your own." (See Chart 2–3 for suggestions on how to introduce mind maps.)

Challenge Project (based on Neihart 1999)

As we discussed, people do not grow intellectually, emotionally, socially, or physically unless they take risks. These risks are not threatening to the health or well-being of the person engaging in the risk, but are designed to push each of us out of our safety zone into an area just beyond our current reach. Think of these principles as you complete the following steps.

Step 1: Choose your challenge focus—educational, physical, or emotional.
Step 2: List five challenges in this area from least challenging to most challenging.
Step 3: Choose one of the five as the challenge you will perform.
Step 4: Create a time line for your completion of the risk.
Step 5: Submit the attached form to your teacher.
Step 6: Complete your challenge.
Step 7: Place artifacts from your challenge in your journal.
Step 8: Write a synopsis of your experience in your journal.
Step 9: Participate in a seminar concerning challenges.

CHALLENGE FOCUS

Five challenges from *least* challenging to *most* challenging:

_____

_____

_____

_____

_____

Circle the challenge you choose to complete.

Share with your parents your choice.

Completion date _____

Parent permission _____

Date _____

Chart 2–2 *Challenge Project*

Mind Maps

PURPOSE:

increase self-awareness, set goals, reflect on content, present current understanding

- Show examples and nonexamples of mind maps.

- Display rubric prominently in the classroom.

- Gather enough plain white paper and colored markers for the entire class.

- Explain the concept that the mind map is exploring.

- Have students brainstorm ideas, images, and connections to the concept.

- Model how to find a personal theme from the initial brainstorming list.

- Refresh student understanding of a metaphor.

- Have them write the theme in the center of the paper.

- Have them continue brainstorming additional words and ideas about their theme.

- Remind students to use color to reflect thinking and insights.

- Have them add symbols and images as appropriate.

- Tell students to show how ideas connect to each other.

Chart 2–3 *Mind Maps*

May be copied for classroom use. © 2009 by John McDermott and Stevi Quate, from Clock Watchers *(Heinemann: Portsmouth, NH).*

Students shared their maps in small groups. They recognized how mind mapping reflected Gardner's research on multiple intelligences and were often surprised at the different ways their classmates thought about the concepts under study. Along with addressing academic goals and continuing to bind them together as a community of learners, the mind maps served another goal. The information on them gave Karen and John insight into students' strengths and needs. For instance, one young woman indicated self-doubt about her ability to write a meaningful essay, and a young man produced an artistic rendering of a revolution that caused the entire class to applaud. John and Karen tucked away this information to use as they supported these learners throughout the year. Karen worked closely with the young woman as she wrote her first essays, building her confidence and praising her competency. Occasionally, John turned to the young man to illustrate on the whiteboard his short lectures, capturing a visual representation of the content that John was teaching. (See Chart 2–4 for the rubric for the mind map assignment.)

At Montbello High School in Denver, Colorado, Olivia Bridges asked her Spanish I students to create a mind map about their culture. The results were displayed throughout the room, and students felt honored by the recognition. Marisela Mosqueda's mind map is shown in Figure 2–5.

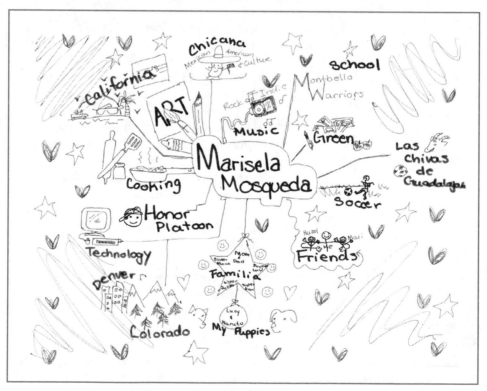

Figure 2–5 *Marisela Mosqueda's Mind Map*

Moves Beyond the Requirements	Meets the Requirements	In Need of Revision
Map shows sophisticated and personal connections among ideas through the use of lines, arrows, symbols, color, and/or drawings and fills the entire space on the paper.	Map shows connections among ideas through lines, symbols, and/or color and fills most of the space on the paper	Map shows few connections among ideas and has a great deal of empty space.
The map has one clear theme clearly and creatively supported by the content of the map.	The map has a central theme and is mostly supported by the content.	There is no clear theme represented by the map.
All words on the map are spelled correctly and graphic representations demonstrate a well-planned design; rough draft is attached.	Most words on the map are spelled correctly and graphic representations demonstrate a well-planned design; rough draft is attached.	Many spelling errors on the map and the graphic representations demonstrate no organization; rough draft is not attached.
A metaphoric representation conveys the main idea.	A metaphoric representation somewhat conveys the main idea.	No metaphoric representation conveys the main idea.

Chart 2–4   *Mind Map Rubric*

▶ Injecting Some Humor: The Magic Box

Knowing that humor builds community along with serving the cognitive purpose of activating memory, Karen and John occasionally produced the Magic Box after a challenging reading. Inside the box was a hodgepodge of items, from extension cords and staplers to children's toys and eating utensils. Students would blindly reach in the box and grab an item. Once all the students had an object, each wrote an informal paper explaining how the object was a metaphor for ideas in the reading. They shared their answers first in small groups and later with the entire class. Some answers were profound while some were certainly a mental stretch; however, laughter filled the classroom. Brandon, the football player who had worried about succeeding in the class, began to understand that learning could be engaging. This helped him understand the ideas from the reading and draw from that confidence when it was time to write an essay.

By not separating the emotional from the academic, Karen and John made laughter a norm. According to David Sousa (1999), humor can increase learning up to 50 percent. Not only does learning increase, but students perceive the teacher as *real*. However, we're talking about humor only, not sarcasm. Sarcasm, even when you are sure the student doesn't mind, can result in pain, distrust, and apprehension on the part of other students listening to the interchange. Students have told John that when they've seen a teacher speak sarcastically to another student, it has made them wonder when the teacher would do the same thing to them.

▶ Increasing Understanding: Journals

John and Karen also used journals to get to know students academically and personally. They required each student to create a personalized journal. Those students who could not afford one found a journal placed discreetly on their desks. Since Karen and John were convinced that journaling opens the door to understanding students and can also anchor learning, they wanted to make sure that each student had one. Within the pages of their journal, learners wondered, questioned, mused, and represented learning through different perspectives. Throughout the year, students applied class readings to their lives and reinterpreted the readings based on their own perspectives. Additionally, they used their journals to think about events and ideas unrelated to the content of the class but important to their lives.

Twice a month, students turned in their journals. Karen and John responded to each journal entry within two days of collecting them. They read all the entries pertaining to the learning and respected student privacy by not reading any entries marked "private." In their short responses, they honored the students' perspectives, provided immediate feedback about their emerging understanding of the course content, and continued to challenge the students. But most importantly they gathered background information concerning students' skills, learning styles, and interests. This information helped them continue to establish trust with their students. Intentionally, Karen and John avoided mentioning grades. At first, students pestered them about their grades. Karen and John's standard response was "Are we about grades or learning?" Eventually questions about grading disappeared.

Through this intentional creation of a caring classroom community, Karen and John were able to build the environment that led to success for students like Brandon. For one of the first times in his high school experience, Brandon knew what it was to be motivated to learn and engaged in his learning. Because of that supportive environment where he was held to high standards, Brandon grew and developed that sense of efficacy so necessary for ongoing learning.

The foundation of learning in any classroom relies on the creation of the caring classroom community. As every homeowner knows, repairing the developing cracks in the foundation or shoring up the shifting nature of the immediate environment will ensure the longevity of a person's most important purchase. This is also true in the classroom. Nothing is more important than our students' learning. The excellent teacher notices any weaknesses in the caring classroom foundation and immediately addresses the problems so uninterrupted learning flourishes in the classroom.

But we know that a caring classroom community isn't enough. Other structures are added to the foundation to provide the complete learning experience. Too often we've seen classrooms where teachers cared but students still weren't engaged. What's the difference between Karen and John's classroom community and those where students aren't engaged? We'll explore this in the following chapters.

Monitoring Yourself

As demonstrated in the stories in this chapter, the development of a community of learners requires more than team-building activities at the start of the year. Students need to work in an environment where they are expected to take risks in order to learn, understand that there are different ways of learning, and understand the norms of participating in that community. Routines and rituals combine to define the community. Unusual assignments, such as mind maps and the

Magic Box, become important routines that are integral to John and Karen's classroom, just as the unusual way that Annie took roll defined the community of her classroom. Intentionally creating and nurturing the caring classroom community requires careful planning with each unit of study.

We invite you to assess yourself on building a classroom community. We hope that by engaging in this kind of self-assessment, you will celebrate what you are doing well and will develop a plan for strengthening the culture of your classroom for the purpose of heightening motivation and engagement.

For More Information

Following are books to explore if you want more information on how to build a caring classroom community.

Bomer, R. 1995. *Time for Meaning: Crafting Literate Lives in Middle and High School*. Portsmouth, NH: Heinemann.

Charles, C. M. 2008. *Building Classroom Discipline*. Boston: Pearson Education.

Easton, L. B. 2002. *The Other Side of Curriculum: Lessons from Learners*. Portsmouth, NH: Heinemann.

Golub, J. 2000. *Making Learning Happen: Strategies for an Interactive Classroom*. Portsmouth, NH: Heinemann.

Jones, V., and L. Jones. 2007. *Comprehensive Classroom Management: Creating Communities of Support and Solving Problems*. Boston: Pearson Education.

Kobrin, D. 2004. *In There with Kids: Crafting Lessons That Connect with Kids*. Alexandria, VA: ASCD.

Kriete, R., and L. Bechtel. 2002. *The Morning Meeting Book*. Greenfield, MA: Northeast Foundation for Children.

Levine, D. 2002. *Building Classroom Communities: Strategies for Building a Culture of Caring*. Bloomington, IN: National Education Services.

Levine, M. 2002. *A Mind at a Time*. New York: Simon and Schuster.

Olson, C. B. 2003. *The Reading Writing Connection: Strategies for Teaching and Learning in the Secondary Classroom*. Boston: Allyn and Bacon.

Tomlinson, C. A. 1999. *The Differentiated Classroom: Responding to the Needs of All Learners*. Alexandria, VA: ASCD.

Wycoff, J. 1991. *Mind Mapping: Your Personal Guide to Exploring Creativity and Problem Solving*. New York: Berkeley Books.

Checking In and Checking Out

*If I have the belief that I can do it, I shall
surely acquire the capacity to do it even
if I may not have it at the beginning.*

—Mahatma Gandhi

Stevi laughs when she thinks about some of the decisions she made early in her career. "I often would have my students write their own tests. I told them this would help them review what we had studied, but the truth was that I hadn't yet written the test and thought I was clever by having them do my work."

At this early point in her career, she had no idea assessments could motivate and engage students. In fact, she thought they had the opposite effect. "It was hard for me to erase from my memory a serious case of text anxiety I once had in college. On that one day I couldn't follow my regular routine of cramming hard the day before a major test. For some reason, I panicked over the test even though I had been keeping up on my reading. Still I couldn't study and couldn't concentrate. When I walked into the classroom to take the test, I was certain that I would fail." Even though she doesn't remember how she did on that test, she does recall the emotional side of the testing situation as if it occurred just last week. It wasn't until she had taught a few years and started using portfolios that she had a hint about the power of assessment to motivate and engage.

While working on this chapter, Stevi was rummaging through her files of student work and found a reflection in a former student's portfolio. Written long ago, Mandy Paal's comments were in stark contrast to Stevi's experience with test anxiety:

> Well, to wrap up this semester of British Literature, I can say I really built my schema. I learned a lot in this class. . . . I enjoyed this class. . . . With all of your compliments on my work, you made me do much better as an individual and I have now changed my mind on English. I actually like it.

In Mandy's portfolio, Stevi found other reflections Mandy had written about her struggles and joys of coming to understand the world of Chaucer and Shakespeare. Stevi noted how Mandy had grown more comfortable with Shakespeare's language and how Mandy had navigated her learning:

> The last papers we were to write with the discussion group and all the poems we had to read and write about were the ultimate test from me. . . . I am glad I am through with these because for the time, as you'll recall, I absolutely hated them and they made me so frustrated I nearly cried. I reread each poem and the diary over about four times, so they sounded as if I knew what I am talking about.

Mandy's portfolio was filled with evidence of engagement in the difficult concepts throughout the course, a course she didn't plan on liking. In addition, Stevi found evidence of how she had tracked and bolstered Mandy's growth by providing feedback on her essays and regularly conferring with her. The portfolio documented how Mandy had grown and how Stevi had supported her progress as a learner.

This wasn't the assessment system that Stevi knew when she first began teaching. Gone was the creation of the test at the last minute. In fact, gone was the idea of a test as the primary assessment tool. And as a result, it was unlikely with this assessment system that Mandy could have crammed for the test at the very end of the unit. Instead, the system itself led to the development of a confident student of literature who was motivated and engaged in her learning. Mandy's story, as told through her portfolio, illustrated the quote from Gandhi that opens this chapter: she developed the belief that she could learn and acquired the capacity to do so.

Assessment: Unlived Potential?

Assessment is one of those educational topics that has its day in the sun and then fades away from the scene. Since the advent of No Child Left Behind and high-stakes testing, assessment is once more in the sun. In fact, it's a topic blistering in the blazing sunlight. In this decade alone, educators have explored formative and summative assessment, benchmark tests, common assessments, assessments for progress monitoring, valid and reliable reading assessments, high-stakes testing, and assessment literacy. They have gathered data, engaged in data dialogues, and defined trends. Indeed, assessment is a scalding hot topic.

Despite the fervor around assessments, we have noted a growing cynicism. One teacher said, "I can make pretty little charts based on the assessment, but who cares? No one ever does a damned thing with them." This teacher, like many others, sees the attention on assessments as a bureaucratic hoop to jump through to please the district office. The mandated assessments too often have morphed into placebos for the state test, and many teachers aren't buying into this. "It's just another way of bowing to the state," one teacher commented, "and that's a game I'm through playing."

Yet formative assessment, when done well, has the power to "double the speed of student learning" (Wiliam 2007–8, 36). But if the result of those assessments is to make another "pretty little chart," it's unlikely that anyone's learning will be doubled. As long as *assessment* is code for *high-stakes testing*, the term is problematic; however, the concept of assessment is robust. It's for this reason that we have shifted our language as we talk about assessment. Instead we talk about checking in with learners to see what students understand and can do, or we talk about checking out learners' understanding to see if they actually got it.

Checking in is what Stevi did as her daughter-in-law, Theresa, trained for the San Francisco marathon. "I used to call her just to check in to see how she was doing. Those phone calls were my way of supporting her while she was working toward this goal. Sometimes Theresa would tell me how nervous she was about the marathon and I saw my role as cheering her on. At other times, she'd confess that she had skipped a few days of running. I knew that by asking her questions, she'd be back in training soon. These check-in phone calls were also a way of saying that I had confidence in her reaching her goal, but more importantly I wanted to make sure she had confidence in her own abilities to complete the marathon." When Theresa returned from San Francisco, Stevi called to check out her results. Did she finish? Yes. What was her time? It was a very respectable time. Together they celebrated her success.

Checking in with students while they're mastering difficult content or developing new skills is similar to those early phone calls: a way of monitoring growth, providing strategies that will buoy learners' confidence, and cheering them on when their confidence slumps. Checking in is the teacher's way of bringing

Gandhi's quote to life: making sure that learners have the belief in themselves and acquire the skills to succeed.

Once the race is done or the unit ends, it's time to check out the progress. Did the student learn? Did the learner perform? Did the student reach her goals? Checking in answers the questions: What do learners understand right now? and What can they do at this moment? Checking out answers other questions: Did they get it? Can they do it?

Missing from the perspective of assessment as checking in and checking out is the gotcha factor. There are no surprises intended to catch students when they're off base. It's not the carrot-and-stick approach to learning, with rewards and punishments waiting around the corner. Instead, the teacher has structured the process so that there are no surprises—targets are clear, the teacher's role as supporter is explicit, the students' responsibility to work toward those targets is in the open, and even the method for checking out the learning is known from the start.

This approach to assessment eliminates the competition between teacher and learner. John vividly remembers a teacher from his early teaching years. This teacher would enter the staff lounge bragging that half of his students failed his test that day. "This is how I know it was a challenging test. I know I'm doing my job." This teacher wanted to "win" the assessment game by making sure that many of his students failed the test.

But how does the concept of assessment as checking in and checking out fit into motivation and engagement? The answer to this question is best answered by a walk on the theoretical side followed by pictures of practice.

How Does Assessment Motivate and Engage?

In Stevi's early days of teaching, she would have dismissed the question: How does assessment motivate and engage? At least, she would have dismissed half of it. Sure, assessment could motivate students to study and to complete their work—to comply with the demands of schools. But engage? No way.

What she didn't know then was that sound assessment practices can actually support students' belief in their capability to succeed. Assessment, as Stevi knew it, was used to judge students' performance in order to dole out appropriate rewards or punishments, often in the form of a grade. However, students don't thrive in environments in which they feel judged. Instead, they thrive in supportive, challenging environments, particularly when they have someone to mentor them (Dweck 2006).

This is where a more compelling vision of assessment enters the picture. Stiggins argues that this new vision "can tap the wellspring of confidence, motivation, and learning potential that resides within every student" (2007, 22). He explains:

> From the very earliest grades, some students learned a great deal very quickly and consistently scored high on assessments. The emotional effect of this was to help them to see themselves as capable learners, and so these students became increasingly confident in school. That confidence gave them the inner emotional strength to take the risk of striving for more success because they believed that success was within their reach. Driven forward by this optimism, these students continued to try hard, and that effort continued to result in success for them. They became the academic and emotional winners. Notice that the trigger for their emotional strength and their learning success was their perception of their success on formal and informal assessments. (2005, 325)

This view of assessment addresses the important concept of self-efficacy, which is directly tied to engagement (Bandura 1997). Without confidence that effort would lead to success, it's unlikely a learner would invest the effort to work hard (Smith and Wilhelm 2006). A return to Csikszentmihalyi's concept of flow continues to explain. People are more willing to exert the energy needed to enter a state of flow if they are confident that they have the skills necessary to be competent in that activity. If they doubt their competency, they're likely to avoid the task altogether.

Enough with the theory. Let's look at a few real-life examples.

Pictures of Practice

Both Kara Kurtz and Nancy Schanke shared many characteristics despite very different teaching situations. Kara taught rural ninth graders who had struggled as readers their entire lives while Nancy taught in an urban charter school. Both came into teaching late, Kara after raising her boys and Nancy after a successful career as an engineer. Both loved the challenges of teaching and were eager to grow in their craft, and both ran a classroom that pulsed with care and challenge. And both learned early in their careers the power of assessment as a motivator and engager.

Since Kara's students had struggled as readers from their early days in school, their idea of fun did not include being in another class for struggling readers. Through assessment, Kara turned them around. "I regularly assess them and show them how much they have grown. What they need is lots of evidence that their hard work makes a difference. They need frequent reminders that they are growing as readers, especially since they've had so many reminders of their failures. My job is to build their confidence. Assessment helps me do just that."

Kara's literacy classroom was filled with posters of bar graphs she had made. These graphs served as cues for what was possible. For instance, one bar graph contrasted how many words per minute students could read at various times throughout the year, dramatically illustrating a tale of growth. Another chart revealed what students knew at the start of their study of prefixes and suffixes. Students knew that this graph would be amended to show their growth after the upcoming test. Kara's walls showed students that success was within their reach. (See Figure 3–1.)

Nancy Schanke credited much of her students' success to a series of staff development courses. From them, she learned the muscle power behind effective assessment practices. Her journal, her instructional coaches' notes, and her grade book provided evidence of her success. In her journal, she told how apprehensive she was as she prepared her students to take that first pre-assessment seriously. She made a deal with them: "Any of the questions that all of you get right will be skipped on the homework. I know that there are questions all of you know, so just think how this is going to make sure you have less homework each night. And any of you who score 95 percent or better won't have to take the post-assessment—unless you

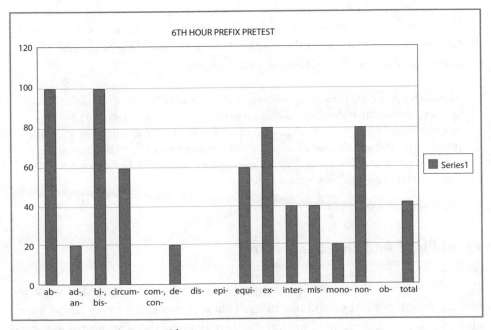

Figure 3–1 *Kara's Pretest Chart*

want to." The day following the pretest, the sixth graders marched into class eager to know how they did. When Nancy explained that there were two problems they all got right, the class cheered.

On the day of the post-assessment, a buzz of excitement filled the air that even Nancy's coach in the back of the room noted. Students were excited—yes, excited—to take the post-assessment. But right before Nancy could hand out the test, drama swept through the room. Crawling between several desks was a huge wolf spider nearly two inches long. A handful of students jumped out of their seats, hollering for help. Other students screamed, and the room was filled with chaos. Finally three students helped Nancy corral the spider into a trash can and remove it from the room. The students calmed down, and Nancy handed out the post-assessment.

And the impact on the post-assessment? Nancy's coach, Pauline Dowdy, tells the rest of the story:

> Due to the invasion of the spider, the bell rang before the students had time to fin-ish; the bell seemed to catch all of them off guard; they were all so focused. Sev-eral students said they didn't want to leave the class, which is wonderful enough but especially powerful since they were leaving to go to lunch. When a class would rather stay with the activity instead of eat, you know the teacher has created a very special environment. I am happy to have witnessed such a connection be-tween students and their teacher.

Nancy and her students were sold on the power of pre- and post-assessments. In her journal, she connected the assessments to the building of a sense of com-petence, so necessary for motivation and engagement:

> The sixth grade class is made up of on-grade level and below math students. They all feel confident that they have a chance to excel, and maybe make a 95% and get to only do half of the homework. But they all *know* that there will be at least one problem on the pretest that all of them will get right and hence be exempt from it on the homework!! So, every day, as soon as I am assigning the homework, their first question is which problems do they not need to do.

Plan! Plan! And Plan Some More!

Recently Stevi met with Jennifer, a second-year teacher, who discussed what she had learned in her first year of teaching. "That year was a nightmare. I was barely able to keep up. Almost all of my lessons were done by the seat of my pants, and the results were predictable. Students were unruly, out of control, and my classroom was chaotic. What did I learn? I learned that I needed to plan, plan, and plan some more." Jennifer was right. If teachers want to capitalize on the power of assessment, they need to plan diligently. Planning is what Nancy credited with her students' success. A look at her process provides a sound model for how to plan.

Nancy's first step in the planning process was right out of the textbook: she determined the learning targets for her unit. These targets were based on the school's math curriculum as well as Nancy's analysis of the state assessment. She wanted students to "read and construct displays of data using appropriate techniques (line graphs, circle graphs, scatter plots, box plots, stem-and-leaf plots) and appropriate technology." Nancy was smart about setting this as her learning target. Because this was a skill that adults used in the world outside of school, it met important criteria for selecting learning targets by focusing on big ideas that would stand students well throughout their lives (Wiggins and McTighe 2005; Stiggins 2001).

Once clear on her learning targets, Nancy thought about her pre- and post-assessments. Fortunately, her math curriculum came with assessments that would work well. But she also needed to help students know what performance criteria she had set. By developing a rubric in student-friendly language, Nancy ensured that all of her students would understand the expectations for success.

Nancy's planning moved on to address how she would involve students in the assessment process. She wanted to make sure she was designing an assessment system that did more than check out what students had learned. She wanted to make sure that her design included assessments *for* learning (Stiggins 2005). That meant that she had to not only think about formative assessments but also figure out ways of ensuring that students were part of the assessment process. She wanted them to regularly reflect on how close they were to reaching the learning targets and be able to explain to someone else what they needed to do to close the gap between what they were able to do on one day and what they needed to do by the end of the unit.

To bring students into the assessment process, Nancy decided to move them into groups that were as heterogeneous as possible. Each person in the group would be assigned a role (see Chapter 5 for more information on setting up groups). One role, important for assessment purposes, was the recorder, who would track the group's progress. This tracking would include not only the answers to problems but also a recounting of the processes used to solve problems. She hoped that by tracking their learning, groups would recognize how they were partners in the assessment process. Thinking of assessment through the lens of partnership has the potential for building a sense of control and competency, so needed for student engagement (Csikszentmihalyi 1997).

Nancy knew that her planning had to include feedback so that students would receive the kind of instruction that would move them closer to meeting the learning targets. To make sure that she could offer them timely and immediate feedback, she knew that the recorder's notes would be an invaluable tool. She also planned to actively monitor individuals' progress. She did this through observations and frequent quizzes. As she planned, she built in time to work closely with students or groups falling behind so she could reteach concepts.

Once the assessment pieces were in place, Nancy figured out the routines and rituals that would lead to success. On most days, class would begin with direct instruction on the learning points of the day. At regular intervals throughout the unit, students would then work with their teams to complete a set of problems. During the last part of the class, Nancy would randomly call on team members to complete one of the problems on the board and explain the process they used for solving the problem. Interspersed throughout the week were quizzes that helped Nancy keep a close eye on individual understanding.

Of course, Nancy's planning included the specific content that students needed to master in order to guarantee success on the postassessment. Before she could determine this content, she needed to be clear about her goals, her routines and rituals, and her means of monitoring student progress. All this planning led to her students wanting to complete their post-assessment even if it meant being late for their lunch.

Pre- and Post-assessments

Stevi's early understanding of assessment was heavy on the gotcha factor. Assessment was a great way of catching students who weren't playing the game of school. Pop quizzes kept them on their toes, and a test with mystery questions was intended to motivate students to study hard. For students with a history of academic success, the gotcha factor is not such a big deal. Many of them think, "Bring it on!" However, for the less secure students, those without a solid background of academic success, the gotcha factor of assessment had the potential of backfiring. For these students the fear of failure or worry about being incompetent can be enough of a reason to disengage (Stiggins 2001, 2005).

An effective pre-assessment has the potential of reducing the gotcha factor by demystifying the learning targets. In fact, for some students, the pre-assessment illuminates what students will do at the end of the unit, providing a glimmer of hope for success. The role of hope as a motivator and engager should not be underestimated. Goleman explains: "Hope, modern researchers are finding, does more than offer a bit of solace amid affliction; it plays a surprisingly potent role in life, offering an advantage in realms as diverse as school achievement and bearing up in onerous jobs" (1995, 97). Hope adds that important quality of building self-confidence needed for engagement.

Nancy's reflections on her first experiences with pre-assessments clearly reveal what happens when students are hopeful that they'll be successful and there is no gotcha factor:

> The most exciting thing about the process is that my students are so engaged in doing the assessment that they won't let me not do it! Even in my lowest class, a few of the students can't wait to take the pretest, since they may become eligible to miss half of the homework till the posttest. Everyone in my gifted seventh-grade class loves it.
>
> I have adapted the process slightly for my eighth-grade students. It is a class made up of eighth grade and below (down to fourth-grade-level math). Several of the students have given up on themselves. Because of that, initially, with my pretest, there were no problems that everyone got right, and there were only two people who got a 95 percent. So, the next unit, I did not do the pretest, thinking that it had only benefited the two students. However, after I saw how great a motivating tool it was for the other two classes, I reinstituted it. This time, again, there were no problems that everyone got right, but I decided to exclude the problem that the least number of people missed (since it was missed by a student who only did part of the test). That has increased motivation.

Kara had similar experiences. However, unlike Nancy, her curriculum did not include two forms of a similar test that could be used as pre- and post-assessments. Instead, Kara had to develop her own. She decided to use the same test to both pre- and post-assess her students. Because her students had histories of struggling on tests, she created graphs that aggregated the results of the assessments. On her graphs, she showed how many students received full credit for each item on the pre-assessment and then after the post-assessment showed the aggregate results for the entire class' success on each of the items.

When It Works, When It Doesn't

David Singer, a math teacher at an inner-city high school in downtown Denver, understood the power of pre- and post-assessments, and so did his students. John had been coaching David for several months, so students knew John. One day, a student greeted him loudly and enthusiastically. "Did you see the chart out in the hall?" John said he had. "Look at what we did! Our average score on the pre was 10 percent. Look at the next graph. Our average score on the post is 80 percent; we are bad!"

Four days earlier, all this young man wanted to talk about was basketball; now he was excited about his math achievements. Talk about engaging assessments.

▶ *Options for Pre-assessments*

Hank, early in his student teaching, was convinced of the value of pre-assessments. The day before he began his unit, he handed out the pre-assessment, which was identical to his post-assessment. "Don't worry if you don't know the answers to these questions. It's not a problem. I just want to see what you know right now."

Students looked at him with chagrin. In not the most appropriate language, one boy blurted out, "How the hell am I supposed to know what this means?"

A girl sitting near him chimed in, "What do you mean you want us to write about our culture? What culture?" She glared at him and then in defiance crumpled up her paper, threw it on the floor, and put her head on her desk. None of Hank's efforts motivated these students to give it a go.

Hank's challenge was highly complex. This group of students had not known much success in school. With 82 percent of students on free and reduced lunch and about 40 percent classified as English language learners, the school reflected the typical story of schools with students from poverty. A good share of them did not have confidence in their academic skills and perceived the pre-assessment as a gotcha despite Hank's best efforts of convincing them otherwise.

When Hank reflected on the student resistance, he realized that the pre-assessment had not been necessary. The unit's post-assessment was to write a personal narrative that explored the role of culture on the students' lives while the learning targets included organization, voice, and style. Since Hank had papers students had already written, he had the information he needed about what students did well as writers and on what skills they needed further support. A new assessment was not necessary since he already had sufficient data about student mastery of his unit's learning targets.

While teaching summer school, Stevi found a different way to determine what students knew and were able to do in relationship to the unit's learning targets. At the conclusion of the unit, students would create a magazine based on the themes in the literature they were studying. Her overarching goal was to have students integrate reading and writing, paying close attention to author's craft. She wanted her students to improve their writing style by using mentor text. She also wanted them to learn a computer program that incorporated photos and illustrations in order to know how to effectively lay out a magazine page. Instead of a traditional pre-assessment, she developed her rubric for the final project and distributed it to students.

"Spend some time reflecting on the rubric. I need to know what you can do right this minute and what you're not sure you can do. As you read the skills listed on the rubric, think about whether or not you could teach someone else how to do that skill. If so, highlight it in yellow. Then those skills that you have no idea about, that you know you can't do at this moment, highlight in blue. My goal is that all of you will earn As or Bs on this assignment, and if I don't know what you can do right now, then I won't know what I need to teach you, so please be as honest as you can."

Stevi was helping students self-assess their current skills. This was similar to what she did at the start of her next unit.

"We're going to be working on multigenre papers, but before we do, I want you to take a look at multigenre papers past students wrote. You'll see that I've marked out their names so you won't recognize your friends. Here's your job. With two other partners, you're going to get a stack of five. Your job is to rank them as good, better, and best. Once you've ranked them, your next task is to determine what made the difference. In other words, you're going to build the criteria for quality for this assignment."

Once the small groups ranked the work and discussed the criteria for quality, they debated their decisions with the entire class. Eventually they arrived at criteria that they could all agree on. On their exit cards for the day, they were to explain where they needed teacher support so that they could achieve the highest grade possible.

Tips for Thinking About Pre- and Post-assessments

From these teachers, we can garner tips for ways to think about pre- and post-assessments if we want to realize the power of these assessments to motivate and engage.

▶ *Bookend the Unit*

Pre- and post-assessments are like bookends to a unit, and like most bookends, the more similar they are, the more effective they are. An analogy is in order here. In the early years of adulthood, Stevi used to use a variety of objects as bookends.

Holding up one end of a stack of books was her husband's bronzed baby shoe while on the other end was a Chianti bottle covered with melted wax. (Does this date her?) The shoe and wine bottle worked as bookends, but they weren't particularly aesthetically pleasing. Now Stevi tends to use matching bookends, which are attractive and practical.

Of course, assessments are not about aesthetics, but for them to be motivating, they do need to match. In other words, both assessments need to assess precisely the same skills, body of knowledge, and concepts. Even though it seems logical that these two assessments actually assess the same learning targets, we have seen teachers unintentionally assess different skills. As an example, a teacher Stevi worked with defined her learning targets for a writing project to include voice and organization. However, in her post-assessment, she included the conventional use of citations. True, this was an important skill; however, it was not one of the learning targets and shifted the post-assessment into a gotcha assessment. Her bookends were similar to the shoe and the wine bottle.

Moreover, the pre- and post-assessments need to be a cognitive and point-value match. If five questions are primarily recall on the pre-assessment, the postassessment needs to include five recall questions. If the learning target is analysis, then both assessments must include the same number of analysis questions.

▶ Provide Incentive

The pre-assessment can work as either an internal or an external motivator. With Nancy's deal of reducing homework, she used the pre-assessments as an external motivator. On the other hand, Kara's approach was more of an internal motivator. Students saw pictures of success daily when they walked in her room. These visual cues provided the incentive many of her students needed to keep on working.

▶ Welcome Students into the Assessment Process

If an intended outcome of assessment is to build a sense of efficacy, students need to be a welcomed partner in the assessment process. Rubrics, then, must be either cowritten with students or written in student-friendly and student-respectful language. Along the way, students need plenty of opportunities to reflect on their strengths, identify their needs, and have a voice in their next steps (Stiggins 2005).

▶ Bring Expectations to Life

A rubric or a description of expectations is one thing, but students need to see models of excellent work. These models could be from a professional, such as mentor text, or from the work of former students. These models provide concrete examples of excellence, which demystifies the assessment process and reduces the gotcha factor.

▶ Stay Flexible

Both Kara and Nancy commented about how pre-assessing students meant that they had to tweak their planning. If students had a strong handle on the content, they knew they would adjust their plans. This way they avoided the frustration Stevi heard from one student when his English teacher announced that they were going to read "The Pit and the Pendulum": "Not again. I've read that every year since seventh grade." Repeating what students already know is not particularly engaging. In fact, you can count on it as a turnoff right from the start.

▶ Honor Both Process and Product

Learning is both about a body of knowledge and the process of constructing that knowledge. Checking in and checking out contains both: checking in on how they're doing and checking out what they know.

▶ Share the Data

Once the pre-assessment is completed, bring in the aggregate data for students to examine. Have them identify the class' strengths, set class goals, and pose solutions for narrowing the gap between where they are as a class and where they want to be at the end of the unit of study.

▶ Celebrate Success

Use the pre-assessment as a reason for celebration. (See Chapter 7 for a more extended discussion of celebration as a way to motivate and engage.) The pre-assessment has the potential of showing not only what students do not know but more importantly what they do know. Kara regularly cheered students forward by reminding them of all that they did bring to the classroom. By reminding students of the challenges they were going to tackle, she helped them see that even if they scored only one question correct, they were doing smart work already.

Kara and Nancy knew the power of celebration. Both graphed student results on pre- and post-assessments. Because of the dramatic increase of scores, the students had reason to celebrate their performance. Kara kept her graphs in her room for students to see while Nancy began posting the results of her assessments in the hall for all to see. Neither one posted student names on the graphs. Instead, they either used codes for students or aggregated the results, showing, for instance, how many students received full credit for each question in the pre-assessment and then the post-assessment. (See Figure 3–2.)

Ongoing Checking In: Providing Feedback

Pre- and post-assessments are, of course, important, but they're not sufficient. In order to take advantage of the motivating power of assessments, teachers need to check in regularly with students throughout the learning journey. Unfortunately, checking in does not guarantee motivation or engagement. Instead, some

Figure 3–2 *Graphs Outside Nancy's Room*

students perceive the checking in as a teacher doubting their capacity (Brookhart 2007–8). Fortunately, we do know ways to think about checking in that are more likely to produce the results that we want. Annie's story serves as a strong illustration of what teachers can do.

▶ Checking In Through Conferences

Even as a student teacher, Annie understood the importance of checking in regularly with students. During a unit on memoir as students were working independently on writing their own, Annie noticed that Jose wasn't working. Instead, he was staring into space. "What's up, Jose? How are you doing?"

"Miss, I don't know what to do. I don't even like to write."

Annie knew that Jose did not feel confident as a writer. A few weeks earlier, she had tried to confer, and he had looked at her with anger. "I'm not stupid, Miss. Just leave me alone." Like many high school students who struggle in school, Jose suspected that Annie was checking in because she thought he was incompetent. Annie knew she had to proceed carefully. "Talk to me, Jose. What's going on?"

"My life's boring. Nothing's happened in it like in those that we read."

Annie suspected that he was stuck on generating ideas, but it wasn't time to move to solutions. She had research to do. "Tell me what you've already tried." Not only did she want to understand his knowledge of the memoir, but she also wanted to understand what strategies he had used to solve his own problem.

"Miss, I don't know. I just can't think of anything to write about."

"Why don't you show me your time line? Let's see if there's anything on it that can help." They looked at it and discussed it for a while. Then Annie remembered an excerpt from Walter Dean Myers' memoir *Bad Boy* (2001). Earlier in the unit, the class had studied short models of well-written memoirs, including excerpts from *Bad Boy*. Annie knew that any feedback she gave him had to be nonevaluative (Ryan and Deci 2000). Any hint of judgment would reignite his feelings of inadequacy.

"This sounds like something Myers wrote about in *Bad Boy*. Do you remember that part? What if you reread it to see how Myers wrote about a similar episode? If that doesn't work, you might try freewriting like we did last week. What do you think?"

Jose decided to revisit Myers, one of the few writers he enjoyed.

Through this short conference, Annie was able to check in with Jose, research his skill level, and then suggest strategies he might try. Because she was nurturing his sense of competence, she wanted him to control his next steps. She might make suggestions, but he was the one to make the final decision on what to do (Brookhart 2007–8). (For more ideas on how to use conferences as a way to check in, see Figure 3–3.)

▶ Checking In Through Teacher Notebooks

One of Annie's tools for checking in during the learning process was her notebook. She had a page dedicated to each student. As she walked around the class, she carried a clipboard with a sheet of large address labels attached to it. When she met with a student for these informal conferences, she jotted down the date, a very brief statement about what she had learned from the student, and the suggestions. At the end of the hour as students were getting ready to move on to the next class, she stuck the labels on the appropriate pages of her notebook. This way she had a system in place to track her students' growth and to make sure that she had checked in with all of them on a regular basis.

"Before I started doing this," she explained one day, "I was certain that I had checked in with all of the students, but I was wrong. There were a few I saw all the time, and a few who had faded into the background. Plus this became a way that I could see what my suggestions had been. With one hundred students daily, I found that I often forgot."

Using Conferences to Check In

Keep in mind that you're teaching the learner, not the assignment.

1. *Research* (Anderson 2000): Ask questions that will lead you to understand the student's perception of her progress and of her struggles. As you research, pay close attention to the student's goals in relationship to the learning targets for the unit. Look for what students do well, especially for struggling students.

2. *Teach:* Once you understand the student's struggles, suggest a strategy or two for moving forward. Think about both content and purpose. What content does the student need to understand, and what learning strategies will support growth? As you decide on what to teach, remember you're teaching for the long run, not just for the assignment. Select teaching points that the student can easily use in the future. But keep options. Suggest several steps and then ask the student what she plans to do.

Figure 3–3 *Using Conferences to Check In*

▶ Getting to Revise

At the end of the memoir unit, Stevi interviewed Annie's students about what they had learned during the unit. What a surprise when she heard several students talk about *getting to* revise their work rather than *having to* revise. Stevi asked the students why they appreciated the opportunity to revise. "Because she showed us what we had to do. And each time that we worked on it, it got better." Checking in regularly was a means for them to learn with Annie. No gotcha factor here. And the students' sense of competency grew in the process.

▶ *Being Intentional About Checking In*

Conferences may be a powerful way to check in with students, but it is only one strategy. Kara used her students' journals as a way to peek into her students' perceptions of their struggles and successes while Nancy frequently used quizzes. Annie read drafts of student work and then conferred with individuals or with groups of students wrestling with similar issues. She also frequently asked students to write exit cards, which were their tickets out of the room. What's important is not the method; rather, it's the intentional checking in that matters. By giving timely feedback, listening to students carefully, and offering options, a teacher can check in and move students closer to success. (See Figure 3–4 for other ways to check in.)

Ways to Check In
Anecdotal notes
Exit cards
Conferences
Quizzes
Team journals
Reflections
Weekly self-assessment by students:
• What have I done well this week?
• What strategies, steps, or practices did I successfully apply this week?

Figure 3–4 *Ways to Check In*

Assessing Your Assessment Practices

Not too long ago, John and Stevi asked teachers to talk about their memories of assessment from middle or high school. One teacher talked about his worst experience: "The test that I remember was in a science class. The test seemed to be written in a foreign language. It had nothing to do with what we had studied. I looked at a friend of mine who was close to hyperventilating. I can still hear him tapping his pencil almost maniacally. It was the last time either of us took a science class by choice." Talk about a test with a gotcha factor—and it was that factor that affected their future interactions with science.

This same teacher contrasted this memory with another one. "I loved [another teacher's] assessments. We got them early and could prepare all that we wanted to. We had the opportunity to show what we knew." By understanding what he was responsible for learning and by having multiple chances for success, this teacher as a high school student acquired the belief in his capacity to learn and to grow.

Isn't that what we want for all our students?

If you'd like more information on how to build a thoughtful check-in–checkout system, we recommend anything by Rick Stiggins, as well as the following title:

Fisher, D., and N. Frey. 2007. *Checking for Understanding: Formative Assessment Techniques for Your Classroom*. Alexandria, VA: ASCD.

Choice

How active, strong, and alert we feel depends a lot on what we do—these feelings become more intense when we are involved with a difficult task, and they get more attenuated when we fail at what we try to do, or when we don't try to do anything. So these feelings can be directly affected by what we choose to do. When we feel active and strong we are also more likely to feel happy, so that in time the choice of what we do will also affect our happiness.

—Mihaly Csikszentmihalyi, *Finding Flow: The Psychology of Optimal Experience*

Ignite Student Passion

They were a good group of guys—nearly always polite and respectful, filled with pride about their budding reputations as athletes, young flirts experimenting with getting the eyes of the girls in the class. As students, they were compliant, doing just enough to keep their Bs. Not a problem, by any means, just not ignited by their work. All that changed with the beginning of the immigration project.

Suzanne introduced the lesson, "Your job is to select a group of immigrants in our area, interview them, and tell their stories. Let's brainstorm possibilities." As the students hollered out the homelands of recent immigrants, Suzanne filled the board: Mexico, Guatemala, Nicaragua, Italy, Sudan, Vietnam, Russia, and

Japan. Once the board was filled, the class listed ideas for finding people to interview: churches and synagogues and monasteries, friends of their families, ethnic festivals. When Suzanne mentioned that there was a Japanese festival the following week, Josh, one of the jocks, shot his hand into the air. "Do you think anyone there was in an internment camp?" During the previous unit on World War II, the passive jock boys' curiosity had been piqued when the class discussed the Japanese-American internment camps.

"I'm not sure, but there certainly might be."

The students moved into groups and began selecting the nationality they wanted to study, generating questions they planned to answer, and developing a draft of a plan. Josh's group was one of the first ones to submit their proposal. All looked great, except that the plan included a trip to the festival Suzanne had mentioned. It would have been fine, but the timing was awful. The festival was in the middle of the school week, and the event they wanted to attend was in the middle of the school day. Because of upcoming district assessments, Suzanne knew that a field trip was out of the question.

"You guys," Suzanne said, shaking her head, "you can't miss school. I can't give you permission to do this. You know the school policy." Josh, now the leader of the group, looked dismayed, but not one to argue, he nodded in understanding and returned to his group to revise the plan.

Or so Suzanne thought.

The following week on the day of the Japanese festival, not a single member of the group was in class. When Suzanne checked the absence list, she saw that all five were excused.

Yes, they had ditched, but later they proudly explained, "We had our parents' permission. Jere's mom even drove us."

Their report was stunning, filled with relevant information that they had gathered at the festival. The details were sharp, and their insights provocative. No longer the passive group of boys who were politely compliant, they exuded energy and passion for the topic in a way Suzanne hadn't seen all year.

Was it right for them to ditch? Of course not. After thinking about the situation, Suzanne concluded, "I wish that I had been wise enough to figure out a sanctioned way for them to attend their independently generated field trip. But I learned a lesson that day. When the work I assigned students included an opportunity for them to make choices so they could pursue a passion and assert their voices, chances increased that they would be motivated to learn."

It's important to weave choice into the curriculum, and we're going to show you how. We'll give you a handful of concrete examples of lessons that include choice and a framework for creating those lessons. But we'll look beyond the classroom to consider two schools where choice was a part of the school culture and created the context that motivated students to show up on a Saturday and after school.

Choice and Motivation

Stevi knew about the importance of choice just by thinking back to her high school experiences. Because she was an avid reader, English classes were right up her alley—that is, until a teacher assigned a novel for the class to read. "You would think that wouldn't be a big deal to me, wouldn't you? After all, I read *1984* twice just for fun and as a fifth grader devoured *Treasure Island*. I used to gravitate toward classics out of choice, but the second a teacher assigned a novel, I resisted. I remember when we were supposed to read *Red Pony* that I just faked my way through it. But the entire time I was faking my way through the book, I was on my third read of *Brave New World*."

Stevi didn't need Csikszentmihalyi's research to tell her how important choice was in order to motivate students to engage in school. On reflection, her experiences informed her of the importance of control and autonomy, particularly for teenagers. As the National Research Council reminds us, "Students will not exert effort in academic work if they are convinced that they lack the capacity to succeed or have no control over outcomes" (2004, 34–35). The report continues:

> In contrast to general values related to education, both experimental and classroom studies tell us a great deal about the specific practices that enhance students' desire to be engaged in intellectual work. Choice is a critical ingredient. Students are more likely to want to do schoolwork when they have some choice in the courses they take, in the material they study, and in the strategies they use to complete tasks. (48)

Choice, according to other research, even has an impact on classroom management. Jim Fay and Foster Cline list choice as a central element in their classroom management system, *Discipline with Love and Logic* (1997). They contend that offering choice allows learners to think for themselves instead of having adults do the thinking for them. The authors also remind teachers of a basic psychological rule: "I either give the other person control on my terms, or he will take control on his terms" (28).

Laying the Foundation

▶ *Creating Purposeful Choice*

Often throughout her career, Stevi experimented with weaving choice into the curriculum, but, like all teachers, she was stymied at times. After all, grading was simpler and planning was more efficient when she made the decisions. But eventually Stevi learned that if she attended more to learning than to teaching, she had to incorporate choice. If Stevi created clear objectives, she could incorporate choice in multiple ways, but it was vital that she was first very clear about the learning goals.

This lesson hit home one semester when Stevi asked students to show in a creative manner what they had learned from reading a novel of their choice. The projects students submitted were indeed creative, but the academic rigor was questionable. One girl spent hours creating a beautiful mobile, but where it was strong in beauty, it was weak in content. Another student proudly displayed a book jacket that he had painstakingly created with a portrait of the main character and a short biography of the author. From studying his book jacket, Stevi couldn't determine if he had read the entire book or just enough to know something about the author and the main character.

After serious reflection on the work she was asking of her students, Stevi realized she had received a hodgepodge of work of little value. Her problem? Lack of clarity around her learning goals. Stevi recognized she did get what she had asked for: creative presentations about students' novels. In future assignments, she learned that the more time she spent determining what students should know and be able to do, the smarter Stevi became at weaving choice into the curriculum that resulted in work that was rigorous, meaningful, and engaging.

In the unit on immigration discussed in the opening vignette, Suzanne's overarching goal was to teach students about authentic research. She wanted students to learn how to enter the world of a researcher by conducting multiple interviews, analyzing the stories they heard to find common threads, and communicating their findings in a way that held the reader's interest. Suzanne also wanted them to accurately document their findings through endnotes and a works cited page. Her job was to teach them how to be successful in this complex task. To reach those goals, there was no reason why Suzanne needed to select the content or make all the decisions. In this project, she determined the goals while the students chose the content and the format of the final product. To guide their choices, Suzanne presented models. Students saw photo-essays, feature articles in themed magazines, multigenre papers similar to what they had completed earlier in the year, digital slide presentations, and digital anthologies. The enthusiasm was palpable in the room as students continued making decisions.

▶ Weaving Choice and Learning Together

Some teachers resist incorporating choice into their instruction because, as one teacher told Stevi, the sky is not the limit: "We have a curriculum to cover. I don't see where I can incorporate choice." As the conversation continued, it became clear that the teacher was interpreting choice broadly. However, as Stevi and the teacher talked about meaningful choice that was clearly hooked to learning goals, the teacher began to relax and see possibilities. They talked about how choice could take several forms: content, process for completing a task, and the product to demonstrate learning.

Choice of Content

When learning goals are broad enough, it's possible to incorporate choice of content into units. During a unit on survival, for instance, students in literature circles selected to read a novel of the group's choice. In a memoir unit, some students looked carefully at memoirs written by musicians while others read memoirs written by teens. On other days students explored mentor texts to study how the authors used dialogue, showed a sense of time, or wrote their leads. The students determined what their focus would be, knowing they would present their findings to the class.

Choice in Process

With the availability of technology, the process for learning is even more complex than in times in the past. When a teacher is clear about her goals, she is able to provide students the flexibility to determine how they will reach the goals. Some students may spend time in the library, exploring books on a topic, while others might conduct personal interviews. Some students might conduct electronic interviews while others might interview neighbors and friends. Of course, there are times when it is important for a student to learn a particular process, but it's the goal that guides the teacher's decisions.

Choice in Product

Katie Gray, a science teacher, is skillful and creative in weaving choice of product into her lessons. She has found Gardner's multiple intelligences to be a useful framework for thinking about choice (see Figure 4–1). "It's all about having

Multiple Intelligences

Visual-Spatial: Learners who like to draw, work with maps, and do puzzles. They enjoy work that is similar to that of an architect. Possible products: charts; models; a video presentation; a graphic novel or nonfiction; reports that incorporate pictures, charts, or graphs; illustrations of concepts

Bodily-Kinesthetic: Learners who need to move and to be active. They enjoy making things, being physical, and participating in hands-on learning. Possible products: a skit, a dance, or a performance in which they demonstrate their learning

Musical: Learners who love music and are attentive to the sounds and rhythms around them. They often enjoy music in the background. Possible products: songs, CD-ROMs with original songs, or multimedia presentations that incorporate music

Intrapersonal: Learners who understand well their own worlds. They often prefer to work alone and can be shy. They are great candidates for independent study. Possible products: essays, creative writing, or individual projects

Linguistic: Learners who love language and are highly expressive. They're the students who love word games, reading, and creative language work. Possible products: essays or creative writing, speeches or recordings of a speech, a mock radio show or podcast, or an advertisement

Logical-Mathematical: Learners who love reasoning and figuring out problems. They tend to think abstractly and conceptually. Possible products: logic games, investigations, or lab reports

Figure 4–1   *Multiple Intelligences*

May be copied for classroom use. © 2009 by John McDermott and Stevi Quate, from Clock Watchers *(Heinemann: Portsmouth, NH).*

clear goals," she explained. "Once I know what the learning targets are, then I can use the seven intelligences as a way to think about how students can show off their learning. There's no reason why everyone needs to write an essay to show me that they understand photosynthesis. I think about the visual-spatial students and encourage them to illustrate the concept. For students who are musical, why not let them write a song and perform it for the class?"

▶ *Providing Just the Right Amount of Choice*

Having clear goals and designing assignments that include choice in content, process, or product are just two steps in the planning process. A teacher also needs to determine the variety of choices appropriate for students. Stevi learned this lesson the hard way. Early in her teaching, she would take students into the library and let them loose to find a novel of their choice. Certain that her struggling students could find a book that would hook them, she was surprised at their reaction. One student after another would demand immediate help. They'd talk for a few minutes until Stevi could lead the student to a section where she might find that good book, but even before she could pull one off the shelf for a preview, another student would loudly declare that he was giving up. "There aren't any good books in here." Others who weren't looking to her for guidance frequently selected a book that was much too difficult for them, guaranteeing that they wouldn't finish it.

Eventually Stevi learned that she needed to narrow the choices for some students but had to be flexible enough to let avid readers select novels they wanted to read. Negotiation was a part of her curriculum, but she learned to make decisions about the range of choice students could successfully handle (Guthrie, Wigfield, and Perencevich 2004).

▶ *Frontloading*

As illustrated previously, sometimes teachers provide choice before students have enough background knowledge to make wise choices. Students need to know just enough about a topic so that they can see opportunities for pursuing an area of interest and know enough so that the teacher can tickle their curiosity. Smith and Wilhelm (2006) refer to frontloading as building that background knowledge.

A few years ago, Stevi and Pam Newman, her social studies teaching partner, wanted students to develop an inquiry project about the ending of World War II. Knowing that the sophomores had limited knowledge about Hiroshima, they created an experience that would engage students both emotionally and intel-lectually. Prior to the start of class, they rearranged the desks so that only a few were in the center of the room, and the desks were facing all four walls. On the walls was a series of large photographs of the bombing of Hiroshima. Before students entered the room, Pam and Stevi dimmed the lights and turned on somber classical music.

As the students came to class, Stevi and Pam stopped them from entering the classroom and moved them into an empty room nearby. There they explained that in small groups, the students were going to visit a photo gallery, and like in other galleries, they were to enter quietly, walk around to study the photographs, and then sit in the chairs in the center of the room to write in their journals. When finished, they were to return to this room so that a new group of students could visit and study the photographs.

At the end of this hour, students were filled with questions about how World War II ended. The gallery experience was sufficient to frontload the information students needed in order to have them make choices for their inquiry projects. (See Figure 4–2 for more ways to frontload.)

Ideas for Frontloading

- Show video clips or excerpts from movies about the theme under study.

- Create an opportunity for students to investigate an element of the topic.

- Play musical selections around the theme and have students generate topics.

- In science, get students to observe and generate questions. (For example, one teacher had students spend an hour watching ants in an ant farm, jotting down observations in their scientific notebooks. From these observations, students generated a series of questions that they used for an inquiry project.)

- Read excerpts from novels that illustrate the theme.

- Give students scenarios that need to be solved. Let students role-play the scenarios and determine an ending. (This works well in social studies, where students predict the outcome of historical events.)

Figure 4–2 *Ideas for Frontloading*

Lesson Examples

Let's take a look at what choice looks like in three classrooms where choice is central. First, we'll take a look at one of John's assignments, called Choices. You'll then see a variation on this assignment called the Sages Grid. We'll then step into Katie Gray's classroom to look closely at her well-structured project Seven Times Seven. From there, we'll challenge you to think about how to add choice to homework assignments.

▶ *Choices*

Early in the school year, John required students to complete an assignment he simply called Choices. Prior to the lesson, he asked students to take a survey about their learning preferences. The survey probed whether they were logical, creative, or experiential learners. The information from the survey served both the students and the teacher well. John gained valuable knowledge about his students as well as initiated them into the routine of choice. Additionally, students saw that their learning preferences could influence their reactions to certain assignments. For instance, a student who leaned toward logical thinking might resist a creative writing task.

Of course, the survey wasn't scientific, but it served the purpose of having students reflect on their learning styles before they decided how they would complete an assignment. Occasionally John would encounter students who claimed to fit all three categories. His response was standard: "Great, you are a well-rounded learner, so it'll be easy for you to make decisions when we have choices for our learning." For the rare student who claimed not to fit any of the categories, John would initiate a discussion concerning how that student learned best.

Once the survey was completed, students moved to the second step. From an options list, students saw the various ways that they could represent their learning. Their job was to select one section and then choose one task from that section. (See Figure 4–3.) A rubric accompanied each task so that students were clear about the expectations. For instance, in a lesson on the political spectrum where John implemented Choices, a sophomore determined that he was an experiential learner. Since it was right before the presidential elections, he decided to develop a survey of the sophomores at the school to determine if they leaned toward the Republican or Democratic Party. He used the descriptors of the political spectrum as the basis of his survey but decided not to identify what was a liberal or a conservative position. To his surprise, many of his friends labeled

Choices Assignment

Place a check mark next to the statements below that describe you.

1. When I purchase an item that needs to be assembled, I enjoy following directions to put it together.
2. I daydream frequently.
3. I enjoy discovering shortcuts to solve a problem.
4. I often need more information when learning something new.
5. I find myself needing a lot of time to think about things.
6. I can "fit in" under most circumstances.
7. I like taking notes.
8. I purposely drive different routes to school (or work), so I don't get bored.
9. I know how to "play the game" with my teachers (or parents); I can usually talk them into anything.
10. Research papers don't bother me.
11. I have a very good sense of humor.
12. I know how to get my friends to help me with my work.
13. I have very high grades.
14. I need to have fun with learning or I don't learn.
15. I know what to say in a job interview.
16. I hate group work.
17. I can't stand lectures.
18. If I had to live on the street, I would survive.
19. I hate making mistakes.
20. People tell me my ideas are "out there."
21. I have to know how the things I learn apply to my life.

Record your responses in the columns below.

Column 1	Column 2	Column 3
Record the total number of check marks for these items.	*Record the total number of check marks for these items.*	*Record the total number of check marks for these items.*
1. _____	2. _____	3. _____
4. _____	5. _____	6. _____
7. _____	8. _____	9. _____
10. _____	11. _____	12. _____
13. _____	14. _____	15. _____
16. _____	17. _____	18. _____
19. _____	20. _____	21. _____
Total _____	Total _____	Total _____

Figure 4–3 *Choices Assignment*

Evaluation

If the total in column 1 is your highest total, you may tend to be a logical learner. If the total in column 2 is your highest total, you may tend to be a creative learner. If the total in column 3 is your highest total, you may tend to be an experiential learner.

Here is the good news: You have a choice for this assignment. Look at Part II: Options. The options are based on different types of learners. Go to the section that matches the type of learner you are, according to the survey results. See if any of these sound interesting to you. If so, choose that one. If you choose one from a different section, no problem; no survey is perfect. The bottom line is it's your choice!

PART II: OPTIONS

Logical Learner: Possibilities

- Take Cornell Notes.
- Create an outline.
- Create a chart representing the information.
- Create a web.
- Write two different points of view on this subject and carefully support each viewpoint.
- Find similarities and differences between the assignment and a different point of view on the issue.

Creative Learner: Possibilities

- Create a drawing representing the topic.
- Write a short play representing the topic.
- Create a game concerning the topic.
- Write a song or a poem concerning the topic.
- Write an extended metaphor for the topic.
- Illustrate and provide dialogue for a cartoon concerning the topic.

Experiential Learner: Possibilities

- Interview a community member interested in the topic.
- Create a survey concerning viewpoints on the issue.
- Find Internet and print sources concerning your assignment and write an editorial for the school newspaper using these resources.
- Create a mind map showing the impact of the assignment topic on the local community.
- Create a poster showing the connection of the topic to a current event.

Figure 4–3 *Continued*

May be copied for classroom use. © 2009 by John McDermott and Stevi Quate, *from* Clock Watchers (*Heinemann: Portsmouth, NH*).

themselves as Republicans, but their surveys revealed a strong preference for liberal perspectives.

The final step in Choices was for students to work in triads to synthesize their learning. Three students, each with a different learning preference, met to share the individual work. While one member of a triad shared, the other members recorded the main ideas. When all three learners completed the process, they synthesized the information by generating a thesis statement about the overall topic.

▶ The Sages Grid

John first developed the Sages Grid while working with an interdisciplinary team. The title of the assignment reflected John's belief that each student had the capacity to be wise or sage-like. Wanting to be intentional about choice and yet clear that there were required assignments in the unit, the team developed a three-column grid. The first column listed the major assignments required of all learners. In the second column students selected a challenge that matched a learning style: mathematical-logical, linguistic, interpersonal, or intrapersonal. Even though John finds Gardner's multiple intelligences theory useful as a way to develop choices, he didn't use all the intelligences in many of his assignments. Instead, he selected those that seemed most relevant to meeting the learning goal.

The third column included options that required students to take their learning out of the classroom and into the world outside of school. Their task was to select one of the options. The work in this column involved family, political organizations, and community issues. After the interdisciplinary team developed choices for each column that led to the goals of the unit, it added a free-choice section for students who had other ideas.

John and his partners, Cindy Calder and Shaun Armour, introduced the Sages Grid on the first day of the unit. They set aside a large block of time for reviewing the choices, answering questions, and setting a due date for students to determine which choices they wanted to do.

Figure 4–4 is an example of a Sages Grid for the unit called Problem Solving. The focus of the unit was the Great Depression. In English, students read the literature of that era, including *The Grapes of Wrath*. In American History, they studied the history of the Depression from the causes of the crash to the impact on society to the steps that led to economic recovery. They also considered the technological developments of the era. Overarching the unit was a problem-solving framework that students used to analyze social, historical, and personal problems.

Unit Assignments	Learning Style	Experiential Learning
Due date:	Due date:	Due date:
Read *Grapes of Wrath* and complete daily activities and assignments. After studying the diverse groups in this period of American history, complete the problem-solving analysis form for three of these groups.	Complete a science or a history problem-solving activity. Begin by identifying the main problem, then offer solutions to the problem and evaluate the solutions based on your own criteria. Be sure to explain in detail the criteria.	Read a book reflecting your cultural heritage. Identify the major problems encountered by the group. Present the information to your family Conduct a seminar with your family concerning the main ideas from the book. Videotape the seminar.
Write an essay integrating *The Great Gatsby* and the history of the 1920s developments of the era. Focus on a major problem in the novel, the historical context of the era, and the hope for the technological development as a means of addressing the problem.	Read a novel concerning technological developments in society. A book report will be required and the format will be supplied by your teacher.	Interview members of American Indian Movement, National Association for the Advancement of Colored People, League of United Latin American Citizens, National Organization for Women, or any other approved ethnic organization concerning how the economy influences them. Present the findings to the school diversity committee.
Learn the material, uncovering the physics of technological development in the 1920s and 1930s.	Choose one of the following books to read and complete the assignments negotiated by you and the teacher. *The Education of Little Tree* *Bury My Heart at Wounded Knee*	Take a risk! Follow the guidelines of the handout provided by your teacher. Through this activity you will learn a new perspective on a negotiated issue related to this unit of study.

Figure 4–4   *Sages Grid: Problem-Solving Unit*   *(continues)*

Unit Assignments	Learning Style	Experiential Learning
Participate in a seminar on problem-solving approaches concerning the role of technology in society, the post-WWI era, and the protagonists of the readings. Reach a conclusion concerning the value of having a problem-solving framework for your personal use.	Do a complete poetry explication. The materials, based on the AP literature test, will be distributed and reviewed.	Research a local problem. Present the different perspectives concerning the issue and write your solution to the problem, based on your own framework for problem solving.
Learn the content presented on the physics of tools that are both simple and complex. Create a Rube Goldberg project based on the rubric distributed by your teacher.	Conduct a seminar on the economic, political, and social implications of depression and recession. Please see your teacher for a complete listing of the seminar requirements.	Organize a field trip to a local farm to simulate the working conditions of migrant workers during the Great Depression. Plan the trip with at least five members of the class. Prepare a report of the experience.
Participate in the Heritage Day celebration.	Free choice! You may choose your assignment. The assignment must be comparable in challenge with the other assignments listed. A written proposal must be submitted and accepted by your teachers.	Free choice! You may choose your assignment. The assignment must be comparable in challenge with the other assignments listed. A written proposal must be submitted and accepted by your teachers.

Figure 4–4 *Continued*

May be copied for classroom use. © 2009 by John McDermott and Stevi Quate, from Clock Watchers *(Heinemann: Portsmouth, NH).*

Some students who struggled in the regular classroom excelled with these choices. Mike was a bright young man who saw little meaning in the day-to-day schoolwork or in the regular homework assignments. When Mike was given choices through the grid, he wrote a mini-symphony for the high school orchestra, complete with different movements. The orchestra performed this piece for the class. After the stunning performance, Mike explained the perspectives of the different movements and how he saw the music related to history; his peers marveled at his brilliance. Another student, who was on the edge of failing, found success by creating a photo-essay of the homeless, representing different perspectives on their plight. Two other girls excelled as well. One wrote and illustrated a children's book about time travel and the connections of historical events. The other organized a Depression-era show, following the model of the 1930s traveling shows, complete with comics, big band music, and swing dancing. These students walked away with a deeper appreciation of history and literature because they had choice in the learning.

▶ Science Times Seven

Near the end of the school year, Katie Gray wanted her science students to investigate a topic about which they felt passionate and to communicate the results of their investigation to the class. Her goals were more open-ended than they would have been earlier in the year. Because she had scaffolded their learning throughout the year by providing opportunities for choice in a tightly structured manner, she wanted to open up options for her honors students.

"I always tried to incorporate the multiple intelligences into my planning, but Science Times Seven offered an opportunity for choice while implementing Gardner's research." Katie spent hours at the computer thinking about her students and what approaches would work for them. She had clear and measurable goals for her learners and wanted evidence of their progress well in advance of the presentation day. She organized her assignment with ample choices, detailed explanations of the assignment, planning worksheets, goal-setting organizers, and rubrics. (See Figure 4–5 for an overview of the assignment. The rest of the support materials are in the appendix on page 139.) On the day of the presentations, students were well prepared. Some students served as audience to the presenting groups. Katie explained, "The students who were audience members were excited to participate because each presenting group included an activity and a discussion in their projects. Not only did the presenting group become experts, but the audience was engaged in learning about each topic."

Science Times Seven

USING THE SEVEN MULTIPLE INTELLIGENCES TO UNDERSTAND SCIENCE

To enhance your understanding of chemistry and general science, your group will design and develop a presentation to educate your classmates and demonstrate your expertise on a particular topic. The presentation will include three sections that promote learning in different ways and your group will utilize at least three of the seven multiple intelligences to make sure that you and your audience members get the most out of each topic.

CHOOSING A TOPIC

Select a chemistry or general science topic that you did not study in middle school science, freshman biology, or Honors Chemistry. Become experts on this topic and develop an innovative way to present it to your classmates. Make sure you choose an area that you are interested in so everyone will have a positive experience. The following list includes some possible chemistry topics:

organic chemistry (structure, function, nomenclature)	petrochemicals
polymers	forms of carbon (diamond, graphite, buckyballs)
chemistry of foods and nutrition	chromatography
electrochemistry	reaction rates
chemistry of beauty (skin care, hair care, perfumes)	environmental chemistry
cellular biochemistry	soaps and detergents
crystalline structure in solids	pharmaceuticals

SECTION 1: INFORMATION (5 MINUTES)

Provide audience members with all of the background information they need to understand your topic. Make sure you give an in-depth explanation of concepts that are involved, instead of just skimming the surface of your topic. You must choose one of the following ways to present the information:

- Design and write a poster and explain it to the audience.
- Write and perform a song or rap

Figure 4–5 *Science Times Seven*

Section 1: *Continued*

- Write and perform a skit.
- Write a poem and read it aloud to the audience.

Section 2: Activity (10–15 minutes)

Invent an activity for audience participation that will help the audience members understand your topic on a deeper level. The activity must be hands-on and it must provide audience members with an opportunity to work together.

Section 3: Discussion (10 minutes)

Find a one-page article that connects your topic to the real world. Facilitate a discussion about the article among audience members, using open-ended questions to get everyone thinking and talking. You must write at least five of these open-ended questions about the article and how it relates to your topic.

Quiz (5–10 minutes)

Write a quiz to assess the audience members' understanding of the topic you presented. The quiz must include at least ten questions that require knowledge, an analysis of information, or skills learned throughout the presentation. Quiz questions can be multiple choice, matching, fill in the blank, or short answer.

Research

You must use five outside resources (other than the discussion article) to support your presentation. Two of them must be hard-copy resources such as encyclopedias, textbooks, magazine articles, or newspaper articles. One must be a database article from our library databases. The other resources may be online journals, credible websites (endorsed by major news organizations or universities), or additional hard-copy resources. You must cite all information that you obtain from these resources and hand in a works cited page that follows MLA style guidelines.

Figure 4–5 *Continued*

May be copied for classroom use. © 2009 by John McDermott and Stevi Quate, from Clock Watchers *(Heinemann: Portsmouth, NH).*

Three of her students chose to go beyond biochemistry into medical technology; they had the audience members pair up to perform laparoscopic surgery in shoe boxes. The audience members took chopsticks as surgical tools, threaded them through a small hole in a shoe box, and placed rubber bands around pins strategically placed in the box. The students had to collaborate because one partner could see the surgery and offer directions while the other partner performed the surgery. Students who participated in the activity were intensely engaged; they wanted to be the first to successfully complete the challenge.

Katie was excited about the results. "The outstanding part of the lesson was how much ownership students took in the learning. They had freedom both in the topic selection and the way they presented the content. The groups felt a lot of pride in their work."

Routines and Rituals: Homework

Nationwide, the completion rate for homework is abysmal. Publications from *Time* magazine to local newspapers indicate few students or parents find the value in homework, even though the research clearly indicates the increase in learning as a result of homework (Marzano 2001). Students are rarely in control of the homework situation; many lack motivation to complete assignments. But what if students had a say in the matter? In Chapter 2, we introduced a choice assignment offering options from each of the multiple intelligences (Chart 2–1). You might recall that the purpose of the assignment was for the teacher—and students—to understand the learners and their various skills. This chart could also be used with homework assignments.

John and his teaching partner, Cindy Calder, gave the assignment a try in two of his classes. In his American History class, students had to read several chapters from *Johnny Got His Gun* and their American History text in preparation for the unit on World War I. John required each student to represent his understanding of the reading through any of the choices on the Multiple Intelligences chart. The homework return rate was surprising: 90 percent of the students handed in their homework. Plus the homework was a delight to read. Linda, who produced a painting that included the sinking of the *Lusitania*, President Wilson, the Black Hand, and Archduke Ferdinand, asked for extra time to complete her assignment. Brian, who sang a song about World War I, performed his rendition in front of the class in a distinctive Bob Dylan style. When Brian produced his first CD years later, he wrote a thank-you on the inside cover to his teachers Cindy and John.

These choices are not for English and social studies teachers alone. When John taught a tenth-grade math class, he offered his students choices for representing their understanding of translations. Jamie, a student who often struggled in the class, handed in the following poem:

> Translation comes in many ways
> Do properties change, or stay the same?
> The slope and distance will help decide
> If the object will turn to one side
> Vertical flips are over the x-axis
> This is a form of translation
> Can you glance once and see the transformation?
> Horizontal flips are over the y-axis,
> But they won't help you do yearly taxes.
> Finding the quadrant a reflected image is in
> Will find new coordinates again and again
> Another type of transformation
> Is doing something called rotation.
> These can be counter clock or clockwise
> but either way it's the same size
> Combined translations move in two places
> and possibly in different spaces.
> To transform a parallelogram
> make a multiplication matrix by hand
> To increase the figures
> multiply but never divide
> The numbers must be more than one
> to make the problem much more fun
> X's are top numbers and Y's are bottom
> MATRICES! Do you got em?

Culture of Choice: Extending Beyond the Classroom

Teachers often complain about students' lack of motivation to do more than the bare requirements; however, this does not have to be the case. At two schools, one a middle-class suburban school and the other an inner-city school with many students of poverty, John and Stevi saw how a school culture that nurtures choice can motivate students to extend their learning day.

The following stories of Super Saturday and After-School Seminars illustrate the power of choice to motivate and engage. After all, how many students are willing to spend their free time on an academic activity? Sure, they'll stay for sports, drama, or band. But to give up a Saturday to present a project or to stay after school to talk about a book? Now that's when you know students are engaged in their learning.

▶ *Super Saturday*

It was a beautiful Saturday in May, and the parking lot at Horizon High School, the suburban high school where John and Stevi taught for more than ten years, was packed. Overflow parking filled the two-lane road that passed in front of the high school. Normally this kind of attraction would be reserved for a basketball or football playoff game. Not today. Family, friends, teachers, neighbors, and administrators gathered to participate in a lesson taught by students.

Inside the doors, students struggled to carry their supplies, contact other members of their group, and register at the check-in tables. Parents, extended family members, neighbors, and friends checked the master schedule displayed in the foyer. The teachers at the check-in table answered questions, handed out folders, and checked presentation schedules for the visitors. Student guides directed people to their destinations. The excitement was clear; Super Saturday was under way once again.

With arms loaded with boxes overflowing with various objects, a pair of students approached the teachers. "Where is our room?" asked Chris, one of the girls.

Nearly in unison, the teachers responded, "What are you doing with all that stuff?"

Chris laughed. "You expect us to do our best; isn't that what you always tell us? Well, this *stuff* is designed for us to reach our goals."

Hundreds of people scrambled to find their destinations through a maze of hallways. For some, it was their first time in a high school classroom after many years. Chris and her partner, Amy, fumbled, juggled, and balanced boxes and construction materials, elbowing their way past rambunctious visitors. They thankfully made it to their room, dropped the materials in a pile, and locked the classroom door behind them.

One hour later, when it was their time to present, visitors entered a transformed environment. The desks were stacked against the walls, and in the middle of the room was a large Native American teepee. Inside the surprisingly large teepee, Chris and Amy were telling Native American stories to a riveted audience ranging in age from five to fifty-five. These two highly gifted girls taught their "students" about the Cheyenne Native American culture through a presentation, a seminar discussing a reading from *Bury My Heart at Wounded Knee* (Brown 2001), and an interactive activity related to their topic. John bounced into the room, took their picture, and smiled with delight.

These girls were two of the five hundred students who participated in the Super Saturday learning extravaganza. Both were sophomores in the required American Studies Program (ASP). All ASP students were required to plan, organize, and implement a lesson on a subject of their choice. Throughout the year, students prepped for their presentation. Eventually they chose their content, decided if they wanted to present individually or in a small group, and developed an outline of their presentation for approval by their teachers. They invited their own audience and created the evaluation form for the audience members. They also had to decide where and when they would teach their lesson. Super Saturday was one choice among many.

Each year attendance at Super Saturday grew, and students began to view the day as a rite of passage even though it was an option. Often at the start of the year, they complained about all they had to do, but at the end of each Super Saturday, students and their parents raved about the experience. The principal's comments captured the mood of the day: "It's the one day of the year when I know I'll only hear good things about our school and our students."

▶ After-School Seminars

It would be easy to dismiss Super Saturday as something that only a suburban school could carry off, but Montbello High School, an inner-city school in Denver, proves otherwise. Even though 74 percent of the students are on free or reduced lunch, students regularly participate voluntarily in an After-School Seminar. Take a look at one of the seminars.

It was 3:30 in the afternoon and twenty-six students and fourteen of their teachers were discussing the novel *Articles of War* (Arvin 2005). The librarian had opened the doors after school for these learners to gather for the seminar while the assistant principal provided food. Student teachers from the local university provided the inspiration, and Montbello students in grades 9–12 engaged in an in-depth discussion of the novel for ninety minutes.

The discussion began with a twelfth grader's question. "Was Heck a coward or a brave man?"

"I don't think he was a coward," a ninth grader responded. "He only did what anyone at this table would do under the same circumstances; he tried to stay alive."

And so began this highly energetic discussion. Young men and women engaged in thoughtful conversation about a confused young man in the middle of World War II. When the ninety minutes were up, the teachers asked the students to write their reactions to the seminar on exit cards. Even though the time was up and they had completed their exit cards, several students stayed on to continue the discussion. They weren't through exploring together Heck's fate.

After the teachers were able to get the students to go home, they read the exit cards:

> I thought the seminar was interesting. I learned so much about the book. . . . I really don't want this to be our last seminar.

> I think that the seminar was really interesting because it gave us the opportunity to hear other people's opinions.

Yes, it was a choice to attend the seminar and a choice to read the novel. And that opportunity to have control over their learning led to the kind of engagement every teacher dreams of. *Of note:* These seminars continue to grow. One year after this seminar, over 90 students attended this optional after-school event.

Why Not Offer Choice?

Asking students to make choices about their education can be risky. They might make poor choices and produce inferior work. They might take on more than they can handle, or they might move in unexpected and unwanted directions. Many teachers are apprehensive about turning over too many decisions to students because of accountability pressures and sometimes lack of trust in their students. After all, teachers need to make sure that students are ready for state assessments, will be able to achieve high scores on the ACT or the SAT, and are meeting the district's or the state's standards. By turning decisions over to students, they are moving into uncharted territory marked by uncertainties. Margaret Wheatley, in her powerful essay "Willing to Be Disturbed," offers a way to think about those fears: "It is very difficult to give up our certainties—our positions, our beliefs, our explanations. These help define us; they lie at the heart of our personal identity. Yet I believe we will succeed in changing this world only if we can think and work together in new ways" (2002, 35).

Consider the curriculum you teach and what you might do next to increase student choice. Whether incorporating meaningful change requires a tweak or a seismic shift in instructional practices, we urge you to take the risk and to see what happens in terms of student engagement. But do give yourself permission to be cautious and weave in just enough choice for you to be comfortable with your decisions. What's important is to take the time to reflect on the results. Are more students engaged? Is the quality of work what you wanted? Are the students meeting your goals? As you see engagement grow and learning deepen, you will gain confidence and the skill at weaving choice into your curriculum so that it makes a difference for the students you teach.

For More Information

The following titles offer more information on how to incorporate choice into your instruction.

Bigelow, T. P., and M. J. Vokoun. 2005. *"What Choice Do I Have?" Reading, Writing, and Speaking Activities to Empower Students*. Portsmouth, NH: Heinemann.

Davis, G. A. 1986. *Creativity Is Forever*. Dubuque, IA: Kendall Hunt.

Ginsberg, M. B., and R. J. Wlodkowski. 2000. *Creating Highly Motivating Classrooms for All Students: A Schoolwide Approach to Powerful Teaching with Diverse Learners*. San Francisco: Jossey-Bass.

Hunter, A., and B. King-Shaver. 2003. *Differentiated Instruction in the English Classroom*. Portsmouth, NH: Heinemann.

Tomlinson, C. A. 1999. *The Differentiated Classroom*. Alexandria, VA: ASCD.

Von Oech, R. 1986. *A Kick in the Seat of the Pants*. New York: Harper and Row.

Collaboration

Introducing Collaboration: Andrea's Story

As a student teacher, Andrea Rodriquez was an advocate of group work. Unfortunately, students in the classroom where she was learning to teach rarely worked together. Instead, seated in rows, they worked independently on teacher-designed tasks. Andrea's supervising teacher explained that students preferred working alone and often were unproductive when working together. Nevertheless she reluctantly let Andrea give group work a go.

Andrea's first attempt might have been her last except for her stubbornness to make it work. All her supervising teacher's warnings predicted the problems she encountered. While Andrea distributed the handout she had prepared the night before, she promised the students, "You're going to enjoy this." But students ignored the promise, barely glanced at the handout, and silently stared straight ahead. They ignored the directions to move into groups, assign roles, and discuss the problem that Andrea had laboriously crafted.

"You have to talk to each other," Andrea cajoled. "All you have to do is to follow the directions on the handout."

The room remained silent. Trying to be patient, Andrea waited and then walked from group to group, urging the students to follow the directions on the handout.

"You only have five minutes left. This is worth twenty points, so you want to make sure that you get started."

Again, there was silence, except in one group. Emily tried to convince her teammates to do the work. When they ignored her, Emily quickly did the work. When the five minutes were up, only Emily had turned in the work; the other students passively accepted the zero.

▶ Six Weeks Later

Six weeks later, Andrea walked into her class and saw that most of the students were already in their groups. Instead of the quiet she had faced that first day, students were getting ready to work. It was a different scene, and one Andrea was proud of. She had learned quite a bit over that month and knew that persistence, careful planning, and diligent modeling had made the difference.

On the second attempt to have students work in groups, Andrea had carefully selected each of the groups and then given each group a limited choice of novels to study. Cesar had been one student she had worried about. Even though Cesar helped select the book his group read, for the first week he proclaimed daily how much he hated reading in general and *that* book in particular. Now Andrea saw him engaging with his group on their presentation. He was leading the discussion about which sections of the novel they were going to highlight.

He wasn't the only student who had gone through some changes. Marcos was encouraging his group to figure out the details of their presentation. Andrea had been surprised to see Marcos assume a leadership role, and so was the special education teacher. "Marcos isn't used to being the leader," the special education teacher had explained. "He's usually fairly passive and disengaged, but he knew he had to step in when the rest of his group was slacking off. He was stressed out a lot until he finally got them to get the work done. Look at him now. I haven't seen such self-confidence since I started working with him." She had worked with Marcos during both his freshman and sophomore years.

Two other boys were in Marcos' and Carlos' group. Often quiet, they had gradually become active participants. Andrea had assumed that the two of them were good friends since they sat near each other and looked to each other for support. "You can only imagine my surprise," Andrea explained, "when I read their first group evaluations to learn that both of them claimed that the best part of being in a group was that they now considered each other 'buddies.' They had not known each other well prior to working in the group."

▶ *How She Got There*

After the initial failure at group work, Andrea was tempted to give up but was determined to make group work succeed. From that painful first experience, she knew she had work to do. Her first step was to be strategic in group membership. Even though students wanted to work with their friends, she knew that she had to make sure each group had someone likely to be a leader and someone who could support the most academically challenged member of the group. Carefully she figured out who would work well with whom and how she could balance student personalities and academic strengths. She also kept her groups to a small size: three or four students. This was enough for good conversation even if students were absent. At the same time, the groups were small enough that there was subtle pressure for all to perform. It was hard to hide in such a small group.

Andrea realized that her students needed to learn how to work collaboratively. Assigning a group task without instruction was a recipe for failure. She began modeling how to work effectively in a group before she moved students into groups. Right before her second attempt at group work, she asked four students to join her in a role play of group work gone bad. One boy agreed to play a sleeping student, another to be the student who did all the work herself, another to get up and wander away from the group, and a fourth to play with his cell phone rather than pay attention to the group. After the simulation and lots of laughter, the class debriefed what the students had observed and together generated a set of agreements for how to work effectively in a group.

But the modeling wasn't enough. Each day that students worked in groups, Andrea started class with a focus lesson on group skills. Her early lessons were devoted to ways that each group member could support effective group processes. Frequently she gave students the language they needed to accomplish their goals. For instance, she helped them figure out how to reconnect to the previous day's learning by using a prompt, such as "Where did we leave off yesterday?" Another focus lesson provided tips for getting team members back on track. Again she gave them the language: "Here's what you might say: 'I'm at the end of the first page; where are you?'" To urge a silent student to talk, she suggested saying, "I'm curious about what you think." She also pushed them to encourage divergent thinking by asking for additional opinions.

Since students were quite familiar with teacher-led instruction, they knew how to comply well. Group work switched the rules, requiring them to take more responsibility for their learning. This switch in paradigms meant that Andrea needed to reinforce new ways of doing school, untypical roles for learners, and unfamiliar ways of making sense of content. To move students from passive, compliant learners to active, engaged learners, Andrea had to model time and time again effective group behavior. Sometimes all she had to do was to ask a leading question, such as "How do you know when everyone in a group is on task?" Often these simple questions led to a change in behaviors.

This required Andrea to monitor student behavior. Daily, she listened to and carefully watched the groups. Without this monitoring, she knew that students would return to their former behavior. In addition, she let students know that they would be graded on their group work. She showed them the rubric (see Chart 5–3 on page 84) and explained that they would be assessing themselves as well as their group members several times during the unit. On the days they were to complete the assessment, she moved them out of their groups and back into rows. Stressing the importance of honesty, she intervened when students were blatantly wrong in their assessment. Her surprise was how more sophisticated the students grew throughout the unit and how much more honest and demanding of each other they were.

From her attempts at making group work effective in her classroom, Andrea distilled her learning into five key points:

1. Good group work needs to be explained and modeled.

2. The teacher must instruct students in strategies for taking an active leadership role.

3. The modeling needs to be repeated when necessary, and students need small reminders about good group work.

4. The teacher must monitor groups.

5. Students grow by assessing themselves as group members and by assessing their group.

Why Go Through the Trouble?

Andrea's persistence at figuring out how to work effectively in groups resulted from her university studies. In her English methods class, she was introduced to the research of the Center for English Learning and Achievement (CELA). In one impressive study, she learned of the difference in student performance between schools that were "beating the odds" and schools where students were performing at the same level as schools with similar demographics (Langer et al. 2000). Students at the high-performing schools worked in small groups more often than students at the other schools. Langer and her colleagues beautifully captured the kind of thinking that resulted: "Minds bump against minds as students interact as both problem-generators and problem-solvers" (14).

In contrast, teachers in the typical schools structured their classes so that students mostly worked independently. On the rare occasion when they worked with others, the expectations were substantively different from the higher-performing schools: "Students may cooperate in completing tasks, but they don't work their conceptualizations through with each other. Often individual students in a group will each complete parts of a worksheet and then exchange answers rather than working and thinking together as a collaborative group" (14).

In another course, Andrea read the research about the importance of student collaboration. She knew that when students work collaboratively, they learn more, are more likely to transfer their learning, and have more positive thoughts about their learning situation than when they work in a more individualistic or competitive environment. In fact, one research report stated, "If you want to raise student achievement, increase the amount of cooperative learning" (Johnson, Johnson, and Roseth 2006, 3).

She also knew the impact collaboration has on motivation and engagement (Guthrie, Wigfield, and Perencevich 2004; Smith and Wilhelm 2006). We are social creatures, after all, and adolescence, as we know, is the time when peers matter. Even Csikszentmihalyi reminds us, "The most positive experiences people report are usually those with friends. This is especially true for adolescents. . . . People are generally much happier and more motivated when with friends, regardless of what they are doing" (1997, 81). But the question is why? Why does working together matter? How does it affect motivation and engagement?

The answers are numerous, but one reason is that there is a social component to self-efficacy. As discussed earlier, self-efficacy refers to the belief that we have ability to accomplish the job at hand. With low self-efficacy, we avoid a task, while with a strong sense of efficacy, we're willing to participate, confident that we'll succeed. One of the ways that students develop that sense of efficacy is by watching their peers. If their peers are successful, the odds are in their favor that they too will succeed. But another reason is that students learn through observation. When they hear the language successful and respected peers use to get the work done, they're likely to use similar language. When they see a successful strategy, they're willing to try this same tactic (Guthrie, Wigfield, and Perencevich 2004).

An obvious example is watching what happens when students text message in class. They watch their friends sneak that phone under the desk and quickly navigate the keyboard to send the message. Often Stevi and John have seen students watching other students perform that secretive task and then follow the leader. They've also overheard students talk about secrets they've learned around text messaging—shortcuts in messaging, tips for fooling the teacher, and reasons their phones are necessary. Talk about social learning!

Types of Groups

Collaboration takes various forms, from flexible groups that are short-term to long-standing groups, which John and Stevi call coaching groups. One purpose of the coaching group is to provide the kind of support that coaches provide: encouragement, an occasional prod, modeling, and support. Clearly, not all collaborative activities require long-term commitments. Decisions about grouping arrangements must reflect the learning purpose.

▶ Flexible Groups

When a teacher wants students to focus on skills, flexible groups are appropriate (Tomlinson 1999). The term *flexible*, frequently used in the elementary classroom, stresses that teachers are not returning to the days of bluebirds and buzzards: no more tracking. Instead, these groups are designed to meet the needs of individuals and have an end date. For instance, in her memoir unit, Annie would often call small groups of students to gather in a circle in the back of the room so she could work with them on specific skills. As most of the class worked on their memoirs, she provided direct instruction to students who shared a common need. In these flexible groups, students honed their skills on punctuating dialogue or writing compelling leads, or whatever specific skills the individuals needed.

Occasionally and thoughtfully grouping students with similar skill levels together applies to highly skilled students as well as students with weaker skill sets. John witnessed this firsthand with two sophomore girls. The two girls were far better writers than anyone else in the class. One of the girls had already written a novel and was working on her second; the other young writer handed in assignments unmatched by John's senior AP-level class. When it came to writer's workshop, often John encouraged these two to work together. If they had not had this time together, they would have become frustrated and might have acted arrogantly toward their classmates. Likewise if their classmates had had to work with these two gifted writers on a regular basis, they could have become frustrated and humiliated.

John has two favorite ways that he uses flexible groups: 4-2-1 and coaching partners. Both activities work well, especially for teachers who are apprehensive about putting students into groups. John learned this while coaching a math teacher who was dead set against grouping students. The teacher argued that students ride on the coattails of their peers and that he would have no way of monitoring the understanding of each individual. John invited him to try 4-2-1, and reluctantly the math teacher agreed. A week later when John met again with him, John found an enthusiastic advocate of group work.

4-2-1

The instructional activity 4-2-1 provides social support while moving students to independence. Students collaborate and yet are accountable for the learning. Riding on the coattails of their peers is difficult.

1. Start with a group of four. In that group, students work on a problem-solving activity or some kind of challenging task. Warn them that they will individually produce their own work at the end of the class. Be sure to give students a specific amount of time to work in this group of four.

2. When the time is up, the group of four splits up and each person finds one other person from a different group to work with. This new pair continues the work on the task for a specified amount of time or works on a new problem similar to the original one but just a bit more complex. Again, provide them a limited amount of time to work together.

3. At the end of that time, students work individually to produce their own answer to a similar task.

When Stevi wanted students to learn the meaning of common prefixes, she followed the 4-2-1 process. At the start of the class, she moved students into groups of four and gave them a list of the prefixes and sentences containing words that began with the prefixes. Their task was to define each prefix. After thirteen minutes (you'll see why she used an odd amount of time later in the chapter), she moved them out of the larger groups and into pairs. With their new partner, students compared their answers and made up their own words that began with each of the prefixes. At the end of eleven minutes, Stevi moved them apart to work independently. This time she gave students a series of new words that began with the prefixes. Their task was to define those words. This last task was their ticket out of the room.

Coaching Partners

When a class was not working in coaching groups, John frequently would assign each student a coaching partner. The goal of the coaching partner, just like the goal of the coaching group (described in the following section), is to ensure that the buddy learns the content. Several times during the class period, coaching partners would meet to summarize the lecture and to quiz each other on the content. For instance, when students were studying the political spectrum, John moved students into coaching partners. Together the pair clarified definitions, generated examples, and quizzed each other. The following day, students took a quiz over the content after a fast review with their coaching partners. After the students received their graded quizzes back, many with higher scores than usual, John saw partners high-fiving each other. For more ideas on grouping students, see Figure 5–1.

▶ Coaching Groups

Selecting Membership for Coaching Groups

As Andrea learned the hard way, teachers need to be thoughtful about group membership in coaching groups. Like Andrea, we prefer groups to be three to four

---

Other Ways for Students to Work Together

Other ways for students to work together:

- *Reviewing a Prior Lesson:* Have pairs list as many details from the previous class that they can recall.

- *Frontloading:* Provide a provocative question around the topic of the day's class. Have students in pairs or triads generate possible answers to the question. (For instance, if the class is about to study *Brown v. Board of Education*, have them define separate but equal.)

- *Summarizing:* Have pairs or triads summarize a lecture or a video.

- *Problem Solving:* Present a problem and have small groups generate solutions as quickly as possible. (An example of this is the troubleshooting group referred to earlier in the chapter.)

- *Observing:* As students watch a video, assign each person in a triad something different to notice: use of colors, camera angles, and lighting.

Figure 5–1   *Other Ways for Students to Work Together*

students. Groups larger than four aren't nearly as productive as smaller groups (Johnson, Johnson, and Roseth 2006). The only exception is in a school with a high absentee rate. One of Stevi's tricks was to add the heaviest absentee offenders to groups as the last step in figuring out group membership. By distributing the absentee students randomly and evenly among the groups, she was able to make sure they had a home when they were present, but the group membership was stable enough for the group to be productive when the offenders were absent.

Both of us prefer heterogeneously-based membership for coaching groups. The research is fairly clear that this type of grouping best serves academic goals. Academically dependent students observe models of more proficient learners at work. Remember the student in Chapter 2 who wanted to drop out of John's class because he was sure he wouldn't be successful? By watching his teammates prepare for seminars and other projects, he picked up the skills and language needed for success. If he had been working only with students with skills that matched his, he would not have been immersed in models of thinking.

Even as we write this, we can hear the voices of parents of our gifted kids: "Why does my child have to be responsible for the work of those who aren't as motivated? My daughter is tired of being everyone's teacher." What's important to keep in mind is that we are not advocating that all grouping be heterogeneous. Instead, we do see times when students with similar skills sets need to work together; however, we live in a collaborative world, and it's important for students to learn to work with students who are different than they are. Carol Ann Tomlinson argues persuasively:

> To address the various learning needs that make up the whole, teacher and students work together in a variety of ways. They use materials flexibly and employ flexible pacing. Sometimes the entire class works together, but sometimes small groups are more effective. . . . Sometimes [the teacher] places students of differing readiness, interests, or learning profiles together. Sometimes assignment to tasks is random. Sometimes the teacher is the primary helper of students. Sometimes students are one another's best source of help. (1999, 13)

Clearly, the gifted learners benefit from coaching groups when these groups are embedded in an intentional flexible grouping strategy.

If a teacher has done everything possible to get to know students, one way of building coaching groups is by identifying various students' talents and unique skills. For instance, Stevi recalls Randy, a boy who struggled with reading but was a talented artist. She made sure he was placed in a group where his artwork could be seen as an asset. In another situation, Josie struggled with spelling and was painfully shy, but she was transformed when she sat in front of a piano. Her group frequently included Josie's musical talents in their presentations. See Figure 5–2 for the process that Stevi uses for building heterogeneous groups.

Building Agreements for Collaboration

As a first step in working collaboratively, have coaching groups develop agreements for how they will work together. Stevi did this by asking students to write in their journals about a time when a group was particularly effective. "This could

A Process for Building Heterogeneous Coaching Groups

1. Make a list of students in the class and set up three columns. In column 1, list the assets each student would bring to a group. These assets might be talents, special skills, or interests. In column 2, list the challenges a student might present to a group. Those challenges could be shyness, dominance, or absenteeism.

2. Using either test data, classroom data, or other data, do a rough ranking of students from perceived academic strengths to weakest strengths. Know that this is just a rough ranking.

3. Build groups of four by assigning the most skilled student, the least skilled one, and two middle students to a group. Continue through the list in this manner until all students are in groups of four; however, do not include any of the students with absentee issues at this point.

4. Once you have a first round of possible groups, add the students who are frequently absent. Many of the groups will now consist of five students: four students who regularly attend and one student who occasionally attends.

5. Study the data in the assets column, and shift students around to ensure that each group has a rough balance of different talents, interests, or skills.

6. Shift students around when you know that there is a potential for problems or to achieve more balance. For instance, if you notice that one group has mostly shy students, switch one of the shy students with someone who is more verbal.

7. Study the groups one more time to make sure there is gender and ethnic diversity. If possible, make sure that each person has one ally in the group. In other words, avoid placing one boy in a group with three girls. It's better to have two boys and two girls. If possible, pair up students who are not in the dominant culture so that they have an obvious ally.

Figure 5–2 *A Process for Building Heterogeneous Coaching Groups*

be a group at school, a soccer team, or even a group of church friends," she explained. After they wrote for a few minutes, she asked them to share with other members of their group. After sharing their writing, they listed four or five commonalities in each of their stories.

That's when Stevi turned the tables on them. "Now think about a time or two when group work was miserable and frustrated you." Again they wrote and shared their stories. The third step in the process built from the earlier two journaling episodes. "Based on your discussion, develop a list of four to five agreements that will define how your group will work together. Keep in mind the plan is that this will be the best group you've ever worked with and the group will ensure your success for the next quarter while you're working together. Once the groups determined their working agreements, Stevi collected them, made a copy for each group member, and kept one herself.

Monitoring the Groups

▶ *Teachers as Monitors*

Like Andrea, Stevi knew the importance of monitoring groups. Frequently she would move to a corner of the room to observe the groups, noting what was going well and where students needed more support. When she noticed that problems were cropping up, as they were bound to, she took fifteen or twenty minutes out of the daily schedule to work on those problems. One week, for instance, she noticed what Johnson and Johnson (1998) call "social loafing," a familiar phenomenon to most teachers. Social loafing refers to students not carrying their weight and relying on group members to complete the work at hand. The first time that Stevi saw this, she called the class to attention, letting the students know that they had a problem that they had to address as a community.

"I'm noticing that some of your groups are falling into a common problem—a few group members have become 'social loafers.'" She knew the importance of naming the problem for them (Johnson 2004), and she expected them to use that language in the future. She also wanted to be certain that they knew why this was unacceptable. "Social loafers rely on the rest of the group to do the work and are slacking off, hurting not only themselves academically but also the rest of the group. What happens is the group gets resentful, and the dynamics can easily fall apart. So let's not let that happen. I'm going to move you into triads in order to troubleshoot this problem. In these troubleshooting triads, the three of you will see what solutions you can figure out."

She then divided the class into triads, making sure that the membership of each triad did not include students from the same coaching group. Their task was to brainstorm as many solutions—outrageous and serious—as they could in three and a half minutes.

"I always give them an odd time for group work like this," she explained. "The novelty of the time gets their attention, and then the limited time adds a bit of pressure for them to do the work."

At the end of the time, she listed on the whiteboard the solutions generated by the class and moved students back into their coaching groups. "Now, your job is to look through this list and find three possible solutions for the next time this happens, two solutions if you need to follow up, and one solution as a last resort This time you have 260 seconds." Once the time was up, students returned to their coaching group to discuss their solutions.

She's used this process on issues other than social loafers. Students have generated solutions to the dominator, the shy student who rarely participates, the nonproducer, and the clown. For a few days following the troubleshooting session, she would have students address specifically what was happening in their groups on their exit slips. Often she'd ask a pointed question, such as "How has your group addressed the issue of the social loafer? What's changed since we held our troubleshooting session on it?"

▶ *Students as Monitors*

Andrea encouraged students to regularly monitor their work as a productive group member through the use of a rubric (Chart 5–3). From the start of working collaboratively, students knew what was on the rubric and that they would be assessing each other. After she modeled good and bad group behavior, students practiced using the rubric to look at the effectiveness of the group processes. For an effective assessment process, she moved students out of the group arrangement and into rows. "When they assessed each other in their groups, they would be 'politically correct' and give each other the same score on the rubric. But the second they were moved away from their groups, scores accurately reflected what happened in their groups."

Stevi had a slightly different plan. Every two weeks or so, she asked the students to take out their agreements and write her a letter. "How well are you holding up your end? What are you doing well and what do you need to do better? And what about your group? Give examples of your successes meeting these agreements and explain one action you all need to get better at." The information in these letters formed the basis for focus lessons on needed group skills.

GROUP WORK RUBRIC

Points	2+	2	1	0
Contributions	Regularly provides useful ideas when participating in the group and in classroom discussion. A definite leader who contributes a lot of effort.	Usually provides useful ideas when participating in the group and in classroom discussion. A strong group member who tries hard!	Sometimes provides useful ideas when participating in the group and in classroom discussion. A satisfactory group member who does what is required.	Rarely provides useful ideas when participating in the group and in classroom discussion. May refuse to participate.
Time Management	Routinely uses time well throughout the project to ensure things get done on time. Group does not have to adjust deadlines or work responsibilities because of this person's procrastination.	Usually uses time well throughout the project but may have procrastinated on one thing. Group does not have to adjust deadlines or work responsibilities because of this person's procrastination.	Tends to procrastinate but always gets things done by the deadlines. Group does not have to adjust deadlines or work responsibilities because of this person's procrastination.	Rarely gets things done by the deadline and the group has to adjust deadlines or work responsibilities because of this person's inadequate time management.
Working with Others	Almost always listens to, shares with, and supports the efforts of others. Tries to keep people working well together.	Usually listens to, shares with, and supports the efforts of others. Does not cause waves in the group.	Often listens to, shares with, and supports the efforts of others, but sometimes is not a good team member.	Rarely listens to, shares with, and supports the efforts of others. Often is not a good team player.
Focus on the Task	Consistently stays focused on the task and what needs to be done. Very self-directed.	Focuses on the task and what needs to be done. Other group members can count on this person.	Focuses on the task and what needs to be done some of the time. Other group members must sometimes nag, prod, and remind to keep this person on task.	Rarely focuses on the task and what needs to be done. Lets others do the work.

Chart 5–3 *Group Work Rubric*

May be copied for classroom use. © *2009 by John McDermott and Stevi Quate, from* Clock Watchers *(Heinemann: Portsmouth, NH).*

Designing the Work of the Group

▶ *Task Considerations*

Just placing students in groups is not sufficient to improve attitude and achievement. This was a lesson Frank was still learning early in his career. Like Andrea, he recognized the potential of collaboration to engage students in their learning. In his sophomore math class, Frank asked his students to regularly work with each other. But the result was uneven. In one section of the room two boys opened their books to do the work and then conversed about the upcoming weekend. When Frank walked by, they would bend over their books and look busy. After he passed them, they returned to their earlier conversation. In another part of the room, four students turned their desks so that they looked like a group, something Frank had asked of them. However, one girl was busy working through the problems while another girl gazed off into the distance. The other two fixed their makeup and gossiped about an event in another class. Toward the middle of the room, a group of four energetically attacked the problems Frank had assigned. When they got stuck, they called Frank over for help and then resumed their conversation. During the thirty minutes of group time, the group was rarely off task. But this could be said only about that group.

Frank's classroom by default highlights the challenges of making collaboration work. Unlike Andrea, he had not trained the students how to work well together. In addition, the orchestration of the group work was a problem. So how could Frank have structured the work so that it had the potential for having an impact?

Interdependence

The students in Frank's class could just as easily have completed their work independently as they could within a group. What Frank didn't understand was that the most effective collaboration occurs when the entire group is needed to successfully reach the goals. Therefore, teachers should assign complex tasks that require the thinking of many people.

Socratic seminars require the kind of thinking we're referring to. Because seminars are built around the importance of exploring ideas and examining differences in opinions, a variety of perspectives are required to be successful. A seminar is successful only when everyone participates. Much has been written about Socratic seminars (Adler 1982, 1983, 1984; Moeller and Moeller 2002), but one interesting variation of the Socratic seminar is the Star Seminar.

For this type of seminar to work well, students typically must have a history working together in coaching groups on a variety of tasks. Prior to the Star Seminar, they should explore a common text, digging in deep to understand the complex ideas and nuances of the text. That text could be an essay, a class novel, a painting, a poem, or nearly anything. What's important is that the group builds a collective understanding of the issues.

On the day of the Star Seminar, the room arrangement is unusual and purposeful. In the center of the room is a circle of desks, enough desks for one representative from each group to sit in the center circle. So if there are five groups in the class, there will be five desks in that center circle. Looking like spokes, straight rows jet out behind each of the center desks. Students from each group sit in the row behind their lead group representative or speaker.

This is the day for the groups to discuss the text in a seminar, but the procedures are slightly different than a typical seminar. As in a regular seminar, the students in the center circle begin the discussion by exploring a meaty question about the text. Again like other seminars, these students are encouraged to refer to the text and to challenge each other by asking questions such as "Where in the text do you find that?" Unlike other seminars, though, the students outside the center circle still have a role. Each student sitting behind the group's representative has a stack of three-by-five-inch index cards. When she thinks of a question or a comment that the group representative in the center circle might ask, she writes the question or comment on a card and passes it up to the center. Since students need to make sure their names are on the cards, the teacher is able to track the participation.

After a set amount of time, usually ten to fifteen minutes, the center circle shifts so that the representative speaker moves to the back of the row and a new group member moves into the center of the circle. In this way all students are expected to participate by moving to the center circle and by posing questions or making additional comments on the three-by-five cards.

Challenge

Collaborative work needs to challenge the learners. Therefore the objective of the work should involve higher-order thinking. Simply completing easy work that could be done alone is unlikely to pull students into the state of flow. Instead, the work needs to be challenging enough that students feel it is worthy of their time and effort. Group work that is easy almost certainly guarantees off-task behavior. In Chapter 6, we explore more about how to weave challenge into the work that students do.

Pacing

When John and Stevi are in their coaching roles, they have the opportunity to observe many different teachers establishing collaborative teams within their classrooms. The novice teachers carefully follow the framework highlighted previously. At the beginning of the class period students are working well and appear to be on their way to meeting the class goals. However, halfway through the period interest begins to wane, students surreptitiously pull out their cell phones, begin social loafing, exchange music on their iPods . . . in short, things fall apart. The issue is nearly always the same: pacing.

Many teachers err on the side of giving too much time for collaborative work. An English teacher John observed allowed her students forty minutes for a task that could be completed in ten minutes. The result was predictable. The students began to work, realized they could be done in a minimum amount of time, and took advantage of the situation. After all, they were teenagers. To make matters worse, when the time had run its course, the teacher asked, "Who needs more time?" Hands went up and the teacher granted them another five minutes.

Contrast this situation to the veteran teacher who announced to his collaborative teams, "You have eight minutes and thirty seconds to solve the math problem in the envelope at your table. Remember your roles established yesterday. Place the solution to your problem on butcher paper and tape your work to the back wall." The teacher started the class timer and the students began feverishly working to accomplish their goal. With three minutes gone, the teacher announced, "You have five minutes and thirty seconds." Students groaned, but renewed energy passed through all teams. Pacing is a critical scaffold for effective collaboration.

▶ *Accountability for Both the Individual and the Group*

If students aren't accountable for their own learning, there's a good chance that some of them will become social loafers. This is one of the concerns that many students and their teachers have. Students who have worked in groups in which this frequently have a negative reaction to group work, and a teacher will have to do more to build their willingness to try it again.

On the other hand, if there is not group accountability, students can move along on their own and not contribute to the group. There are lots of ways of dealing with this, many that you probably already know. We offer three structures that support accountability for both the individual and the group.

Panels
Put students into groups of four or five. Have the students in each group number off. Give them a limited amount of time to work on a specific task. This works best if each group has a slightly different task to work on so that each group can contribute to the knowledge of the entire class. After group work time, randomly call on a representative from each group to form a panel to answer an overarching question.

Here's an example. A class is studying the short story "The Scarlet Ibis." The overarching question is about the significance of the strange bird in the story, the scarlet ibis. Each group has a different charge:

- *Group 1:* Find the symbols and metaphors that reflect pride and love.
- *Group 2:* Trace the changes in the brother from the start of the story to the end of the story.
- *Group 3:* Can you trust the narrator? After all, this is his story told from an adult perspective. Use quotes in the story to support your answer.

Each person in the group has been assigned a number. At the end of the allotted group work time, the teacher randomly selects a number. The person with that number in each group is a member of the panel who then summarizes his group's discussion for the class.

Pair-Share

Before you begin a pair-share activity, write each student's name on a three-by-five card.

1. In pairs, have students answer questions or solve a problem. Do not give them too much time to do this. (Remember the pacing issue we discussed earlier.)
2. Shuffle the cards and draw a student's name. This is the person who answers the first question or states the solution.
3. Return the card to the deck, and shuffle again. (It's important to put the card back because it's the randomness of the card selection that counts. Students need to feel like their name could be called at any time and that there is no such thing as getting off the hook.) Draw another card, and have that student answer the next question, and so on.

Four Heads Are Better Than One

For the teacher who would like to end the period with a class in laughter, the Four Heads Are Better Than One Quiz is guaranteed to achieve this goal.

1. Divide the class into four groups (or more and change the name to the Five Heads Are Better Than One Quiz, or however many groups you have. If your class is set up in coaching groups, then you would select one person per coaching group.)

2. Give each group time to study the content together.

3. Near the end of the class period, have each group count off so that each person has a number.

4. Write down each of the numbers on a slip of paper. For instance, if the largest group has four members, have four slips of paper numbered 1–4.

5. Ask a random student to draw a number from a hat or other container. Then place that number back in the hat.

6. One member per team with that number goes to the front of the room and stands in a row.

7. The teacher asks a question connected to the content the groups have studied.

8. Here's the tricky part: each person in the line contributes to the answer, but each person can say only *one* word, and answers need to be in full sentences.

9. The sentence continues until someone says "period."

10. After the laughter quiets down, each person returns to the home group to discuss how the question could have been answered.

11. The teacher draws another number, and a representative from each group goes to the front of the room for another question.

▶ Grading

And then there is that very messy issue of grading. How does a teacher grade group work so that the grade is equitable and reflects the academic achievement of each student? We've found several strategies that have been effective. But no matter what strategy a teacher selects, one factor is a must: a rubric that accurately defines the outcomes and the quality of the expected work. For this rubric to be effective, students need to collaboratively self-assess and create action plans for ongoing improvement. As we discussed in Chapter 3, student engagement is heightened when students understand the expectations and receive feedback on their progression toward the goals. The rubric along with ongoing self-assessment defines those goals and offers students the chance to make the necessary adjustments along the way.

Some teachers include collaboration as part of the criteria on a rubric. When the outcomes include learning how to work effectively as a group, this is a fair consideration for assessment. Of course, it requires the teacher to monitor how each group is collaborating and provide essential instruction to help the students grow in this area.

Shaun Armour used another method for group work. His rubric focused on the task that students were expected to accomplish. But after the task or project was completed, he asked students to draw a circle, like a pie, and divide the circle into portions that reflected the amount of work that each student contributed to the project. For the student guilty of social loafing, his slice would be slim while the go-getter who did a lion's share of the work would have a much larger slice. Shaun collected these charts and used them to determine how to allocate the points earned on the project. An average of what teammates determined went into the grade book. For example, if a project earned 85 out of 100 points and if the group determined that one student worked half as hard as others, he would earn only half of the 85 points.

Designing group work from the planning stage to the grading stage can be challenging and stressful, especially as the teacher begins this process. However, it's worth the stress because of the payoffs. Johnson and Johnson (1994), highly regarded researchers in cooperative learning, have identified five components needed for effective group work, shown in Figure 5–4.

Research-Based Components of Group Work

The most research on group work has probably been done by the cooperative learning team David and Roger Johnson (1998). According to them, there are five essential components for effective group work:

1. *Positive Interdependence:* This is the sink-or-swim theory: for a group to succeed or to fail, it takes the efforts of each individual within that group.

2. *Face-to-Face Interaction:* Students need to interact with each other. They need to talk, support, encourage, applaud, and think together.

3. *Individual and Group Accountability:* Not only is the group responsible for doing the work, but individuals must be accountable for the quality of their contributions.

4. *Interpersonal and Group Work Skills:* As Andrea found, if students don't have the skills for working collaboratively, they need to learn them.

5. *Group Processing:* Group members need to reflect on how well they are working together and analyze what is working well and what needs improvement.

Figure 5–4   *Research-Based Components of Group Work*

The Class as a Collaborative Community

Marcia, like Andrea at the start of the chapter, had wanted her students to work collaboratively but she hadn't been successful so far. Wanting to give it one more try, she set up her groups in advance to make sure that there was a proper balance of academically strong students and ones with challenges. But immediately problems cropped up.

"Juan, I'd like you to work with Sarah and Jesse."

"Not going to do it! I'm fine here. Besides, I don't even like them."

The more she prodded Juan to move, the more he resisted and the louder he declared his dislike of his two new partners. Finally, he gave in and moved. He announced loudly as he grabbed his backpack and moved across the room, "I'm not doing any work, Miss. It'll be a waste of time." And Juan was right. He defiantly turned his back to his new partners, crossed his arms, and did nothing but show his anger.

This story illustrates that a prerequisite for effective group work is a caring classroom community in which students know each other well enough that they can work together. True, this was a challenging class, but those challenges pointed to the importance of building a safe classroom culture where everyone knew each other well and knew how to collaborate with each other.

This was a lesson that Annie had learned. She knew students did not know each other well and that there were cliques that worked against the classroom culture. Determined to change the culture of the classroom, she worked hard at incorporating meaningful team-building activities. Students wrote poems about themselves and posted them on the walls. They moved into pairs and talked about their memories, all in preparation for writing their memoirs. But what Annie had not expected was the outburst of anger that erupted one day.

Students who hadn't worked closely together were for the first time that year interacting with each other. Prior to these activities, the Latino students had stayed on one side of the room while the white students kept to themselves. When they began working in cross-ethnic groups, tensions flared. Annie didn't know what had caused the first outburst, but she saw its repercussions. "She's prejudiced, Miss," one student angrily yelled. "She doesn't like Mexicans and we don't like her." Racial epitaphs flew across the room before Annie could calm the students down.

For a couple of days, the room was filled with an undercurrent of anger, but Annie continued having students work together, and together the class discussed the anger in the room. Perceived slights and misunderstood comments became public, and the students talked and wrote about their frustration. By the end of those tension-filled classes, the students had calmed down and a sense of community had developed. As a result of working through the tensions, they bonded. When Stevi interviewed this class toward the end of the year, several students referred to this instance. One said, "You should have seen us, Miss. We hated each other. But now we don't. We learned to work together—and we're tight."

It was a tough lesson for Annie and the students, but an important one. Community must be nurtured and cultivated for students to work well with each other, and community brings with it tensions and frustrations. Some of the literature on community discusses the difference between a pseudo-community and an authentic one (Peck 1987). Pseudo-communities are often marked by politeness and avoidance of anything that might disturb the comfort level of the participants. In contrast, authentic communities occasionally are marked by high emotion. Annie's class crossed over from a pseudo-community to an authentic one. As uncomfortable as those days were, they were important for the class to emerge as a classroom community with a culture of collaboration.

Putting It All Together

We want to end this chapter with a picture of a day in Matt Brother's AP Social Studies class. Matt had been the stereotype of the coach who also happened to be a social studies teacher. He lectured, showed videos, and asked students to answer questions at the end of the chapter. But about a decade into his career, he became dissatisfied with his instruction. Working with an instructional coach, Matt changed his practice and fell back in love with teaching, and his students fell in love with learning history and Matt's class.

Matt began to think about his class like he thought about his football team. He wanted active engagement, student collaboration, and obvious student growth. To get this, he knew he had to coach his students and get them to do the thinking. He also knew that he needed to think about his class as if it were a team. Classroom culture mattered, he argued, just like the spirit of a team mattered.

His day often started out with students actively reviewing what they had learned the previous day or as a preview of what they were about to learn that day. Some days he began with a Tea Party, a strategy he learned by reading Kylene Beers (2003). When students walked in the room, he handed them a quote from a reading they were about to engage in. Their task was to wander through the room, find another student to read the quote to, and then discuss it. Next students would exchange quotes and find someone else to talk to about the new quote. After about six minutes, he stopped the Tea Party and had them return to their seats.

On other days he might have students do a Carousel Brainstorm. On large flip charts, he would write questions about content covered in earlier classes. As students walked into the room, he randomly assigned students to groups to begin brainstorming and writing an answer to one of the questions on the flip charts. Then he would have each group move to the next flip chart and work on that question. This would continue until each group had added thinking to each of the flip charts.

By beginning each class period with an activity such as the Tea Party or the Carousel Brainstorm, Matt made sure that each student had his voice in the room and had talked to someone new. "It's like a drill before we play," Matt would explain. "You have to warm them up, get them thinking, and do it in a way that builds a team spirit." Matt made sure that the culture of his classroom was one of collaboration and that there was a palpable caring classroom community.

Following the warm-up, students continued with the learning. Knowing that the text they were reading was often challenging, Matt incorporated a process called reciprocal teaching. Typically used with struggling readers, reciprocal teaching was a strategy that would support even AP readers as they encountered challenging text. Far from struggling, these students were motivated to do well in school but didn't have the strategies in place to navigate the challenging text they encountered in an Advanced Placement class.

Reciprocal teaching is based on students using four thinking strategies while assuming the role of the teacher: questioning, predicting, clarifying, and summarizing. Matt had modeled these strategies with his students and showed them how to think like a teacher before he moved students into groups of four and handed out a challenging text for them to read together. At the end of four to five paragraphs, Matt asked them to stop reading and begin discussing the text. Each person was assigned a role: questioner, summarizer, predictor, or clarifier. When they discussed, their task was to prod their teammates into questioning, predicting, clarifying, or summarizing, depending on their role. Matt had taught them the language of teaching, so they knew to make statements such as "Who has a question concerning what we just read?" And if no one had a question, the questioner might prod more. "What if we took the subheading and turned it into a question. What would that sound like? And how would we answer it?"

Matt had formed the groups intentionally to ensure that there was a mix of students in each group. He assigned them roles and then let them switch the roles every now and then, but each student had something specific to contribute to the group. He explained the goal for the reciprocal teaching to them. Often their goal was to learn some concept or answer a series of higher-order questions once they were through with the text. There was accountability for all: the students were in charge of their particular thinking strategy and received an individual grade on an upcoming quiz over the context. He also gave each group bonus points. The bonus was based on the group's average on the quiz, so the higher the average score, the larger the bonus points.

Matt's class had changed. No longer seeing himself as the disseminator of information, Matt said he had to have his students play the game of learning. "We don't do it alone," he explained. "We have to be a team, just like my football team. And, hey, it's a lot more fun for all of us."

When Matt won the teacher of the year award for his district, he was certain it was because of the changes he had made, but the award was nothing compared with the engagement he saw in his class.

And isn't that what we want for *all* students?

For More Information

Instead of listing books for further study, we urge you to visit the following two websites for more information. Both are chock-full of information on student collaboration.

The Cooperative Learning Center at the University of Minnesota (www.co-operation.org/): Roger and David Johnson's website contains the research and theory behind cooperative learning as well as classroom ideas and solutions to common problems.

Kagan Publishing and Professional Development (www.kaganonline.com/): Spencer Kagan's site, which includes Kagan's structures for cooperative learning.

Challenge

> The best moments usually occur when a person's body or mind is stretched to its limits in a voluntary effort to accomplish something difficult and worthwhile.
>
> —Mihaly Csikszentmihalyi, *Flow: The Psychology of Optimal Experience*

> I like a good challenge—it forces us to think!
>
> —Student 10th Grade

Tina's Story

For an hour each week, teachers gathered together to either learn a new instructional strategy, look at student work, or provide feedback on a teacher's assignment. On this day, Tina agreed to share a future assignment for her tenth-grade advanced literature class. Nadine facilitated.

"Remember," Nadine explained, "we're going to be looking at work from Tina's advanced class. She'll explain it, and then we'll talk about what we liked and what we think could improve the assignment."

"You all know how frustrated I've been," Tina began. "My kids just don't want to work and aren't getting their assignments in. I think this is one assignment, though, that'll work for them. Their job is to pick two characters in the story we're going to read and to have one character write a postcard to the other. I want them to be sure to write in the persona of their selected character. Here's the handout I've created." She passed around a half sheet of paper with an illustration of a postcard on it. There was room for an address and enough space for students to write a paragraph at the most. "I think they'll enjoy this. It'll be a change for them."

"Let's give Tina some feedback, but first what did you like?"

"It's creative."

"The kids should enjoy writing a postcard instead of the typical writing they do in the literature class."

"I like the handout. It's cute and looks like a real postcard."

"Do you have questions or feedback for Tina?"

One teacher, new to the school, looked puzzled and hesitantly asked, "You said this was for an advanced sophomore literature class, I think. Could you talk about how you think about the assignments for this class in contrast to your other literature classes?"

"Sure. In my other classes, I couldn't ask them to do an assignment like this. I'd have to explain and explain along with giving them exact directions for everything they do. With this class, I can give them more open-ended assignments, and they'll take off."

When the group met again, Tina wasn't happy. "The postcard didn't work either. Almost no one turned the assignment in. They are so lazy!"

Tina was caught in the trap of many teachers in high-poverty schools. Convinced that her students couldn't or wouldn't meet the demands of challenging tasks, Tina assigned low-level work that required little effort. Each time students either didn't turn in work or rushed through an assignment, her belief that her students needed more structure or an easier task grew in strength. And students lived up to her low expectations. Bored, they barely paid attention in class, let alone completed the work that Tina asked of them. Engagement was nonexistent in her classroom.

Challenge and Engagement

What Tina didn't understand is that an appropriate level of challenge contributes to engagement. In fact, challenge motivates students to try to do hard stuff, and it's the challenge that engages them in the experience. For Stevi, the importance of challenge became clear when she reflected on learning to ski. At first, she was challenged by the bunny slopes that beginners learn to ski on. Those short, gentle slopes were perfect for learning to control her speed and mastering the snowplow. As she became adept at skiing on bunny slopes, she started getting bored. When a friend suggested that she try the green slopes, one notch up in terms of difficulty, she found herself once again challenged, and the fun returned.

Csikszentmihalyi (1990, 1997) helps us understand why challenge is vital in motivation and engagement. He explains that we enter into the state of flow when the level of challenge matches our current set of skills. However, any mismatch between the two reduces the level of engagement. For instance, when students' skills surpass those needed to complete an assignment, there is a mismatch. This is what happened with Tina's postcard assignment. Her students' writing skills far surpassed the required task. The assignment was like the bunny slope when Stevi had the snowplow under control. Boring!

On the other hand, when students face a task with a high challenge and they don't have the requisite skills, they're anxious, and there's a good chance that trouble's ahead. Just ask Stevi how she felt about skiing the black slopes that advanced skiers gleefully attack! As an intermediate skier, her skill level was inadequate for tackling those slopes. The few times she tried to ski a black slope, she tensed up and skied worse than she was capable of. In fact, she learned clever ways to avoid them. One time when skiing with friends who were much stronger skiers than she, she falsely claimed that she was feeling a bit of vertigo and was going to go hang out in the lodge for a while. She knew a drink would do her good.

Her need to avoid a challenge that was above and beyond her skills was connected to the need to feel competent (Csikszentmihalyi 1997; National Research Council 2004). Remember, engagement involves both emotions and behavior (National Research Council 2004). Stevi's emotional response focused on saving face. She did not want to freeze up on the slope nor did she want to demonstrate her lack of skill to friends she admired. Like Stevi, students want to save face. It's the rare student who wants her social group to see her as incompetent and incapable. As the National Research Council's (2004) study of student engagement points out, students' perceptions of success are directly related to motivation. If they think they'll perform poorly on a task, many of them won't be willing to give it a go. And there's no hope anyone will be engaged in her learning if she doesn't even take that first step. We have to catch them before we can hold them.

Csikszentmihalyi (1997) depicts this relationship of skills and challenge to the flow experience. When skills are low and challenge is high, people often feel anxious. In a classroom, this could be a cause of test anxiety or the nervousness many students feel when they need to give a speech. Csikszentmihalyi further contends that when challenge and skills are low, people are often apathetic. John and Stevi think about this relationship when they visit special education classes or intervention programs at the secondary level. Even though the students are struggling learners, many of their assigned tasks are quite simple and similar to work these students have done in earlier grades. Could that be the reason many of these students are bored?

Recently, Stevi interviewed students about what engaged them. One student explained, "I like a medium challenge." A medium challenge was one that was just right but not too tough. "Something that forces you to think," he added. These students described what Csikszentmihalyi refers to as an optimal experience. It's that level of challenge that pulls students into the activity and that promotes the likelihood of a flow experience.

The optimal experience, one that produces a bit of anxiety with a sense of hope, sets up a dynamic cycle. Because of the challenge, students need to put into action a set of strategies, often new to them. With practice, success grows, and with additional success, they are drawn to new challenges, which in turn require a new set of skills. And so the cycle continues. This cycle is one Stevi recognizes from her early skiing days. After she learned the skills to successfully make it down the bunny slopes, she needed to increase the level of challenge. She headed off for the green slopes. There she perfected the snowplow and began to learn new skills, such as keeping her skis parallel. While learning new skills, she entered the state of flow. Worries about classes and students and lesson plans slipped away, and all that was in her world were the white slopes ahead of her.

Csikszentmihalyi explained this process: "It is this dynamic feature that explains why flow activities lead to growth and discovery. One cannot enjoy doing the same thing at the same level for long. We grow either bored or frustrated; and then the desire to enjoy ourselves again pushes us to stretch our skills, or to discover new opportunities for using them" (1990, 75).

In the Zone

Vygotsky's (1989) zone of proximal development further explains the need to increase the level of challenge in the learning process. This zone metaphorically reflects the distance between what a student can do independently and what she can do with support. Through the assistance of a more capable other or a mentor of some sort, students grow from dependence on that more capable other to independence. Their movement to independence is supported by assisted learning (Tharp and Gallimore 1993). Through modeling, providing explicit directions, asking questions, and offering strategic feedback, the more capable other gradually turns control of the action over to the learner. This assistance is also called scaffolding.

A teacher's goal is to teach just slightly beyond where a student is (Smith and Wilhelm 2002; Vygotsky 1989). This is where engagement is most likely to occur. Consider what happens when we're offered assistance on a task we already know how to do. Stevi, for instance, gets irritated, and John tends to ignore the offer. According to the national study on engagement, if students receive help for work they believe they're capable of doing, they often suspect that their teachers think they are incompetent and incapable of difficult work (National Research Council 2004). On the other hand, if the teacher doesn't provide enough scaffolding, the student begins to feel anxious and may tune out of the learning situation (Smith and Wilhelm 2006).

Let's step into George's classroom and watch how challenge, high expectations, and scaffolding that assisted a student's performance contributed to creating the context in which Adam, a special education student, became engaged in his learning. He certainly didn't start out that way.

George's Story

Arms crossed or staring straight ahead, Adam let George know that he had no interest in social studies. A special education student, Adam trusted that his resource teacher would bail him out, but George was adamant that Adam would participate and learn. Patiently, George would wander to the back of the room, tap Adam on the head, and ask him quietly to join the class discussion.

With the upcoming presidential election year, George framed his curriculum around the issues and activities of the day. When he announced that students were going to participate in a simulated political convention, the students were visibly curious—even Adam. "You'll need to take a position and determine which candidate you're going to back. But taking a position isn't enough; you'll have to back it up. Plus you'll need posters advocating at least one of your positions. And don't forget that delegates dress up a bit. None of those ripped jeans!"

For the next two weeks, students studied the issues that were hot that year. As they read magazine articles and listened to political speeches, they tracked their understanding of the issues in their learning journals or on graphic organizers such as Venn diagrams or T-charts. As much as possible, George brought in accessible and interesting text for them to read. Newspapers from across the nation, magazines such as *Newsweek* and *Time*, and transcripts from talk radio shows filled the room. Students read the news and commentaries and learned how to spot the difference between reporting and editorializing. One assignment required students to listen to radio segments from National Public Radio and Rush Limbaugh and find similarities and differences between their presentations of views on an issue.

Often students quickly honed in on their positions about the issues, but by playing devil's advocate, George pushed them to examine and reexamine their positions. If a student suggested that one candidate's foreign policy position was sound, George argued the opposing position. And then when another student would echo George's professed stance, he would gracefully slide into a new argument, logically contradicting his previous arguments. During this time, Adam listened but rarely participated. No longer was his head on his desk, nor were his arms folded.

When George moved students into small groups to study issues in depth, Adam continued to listen and only occasionally asked questions. George was intentional about the group he assigned Adam to. He wanted the group to be one that would support and nudge Adam. One girl, in particular, had worked well with him, making sure he understood the assignments and further explaining the tasks, as needed.

In their groups, students practiced the behaviors needed for a successful convention. Sometimes, they rehearsed nomination and acceptance speeches. On other days, they critiqued each other's work and offered ideas for the signs.

On the day before the mock convention, George worried about Adam. "I'm not sure he'll be here tomorrow, and if he is, I'm not convinced he'll come prepared." But George was surprised when Adam came in the next day. Not only did he have his homemade sign—with many of the words misspelled but his position clear—but he also had on a suit. Yes, the tail of his shirt was hanging out in back and his tie was askew, but he almost looked like the conventioneer ready to argue a position and cast a vote.

That day was a great one for those watching Adam. The acting side of him trumped the shy side, and the unmotivated guy had morphed into someone highly engaged in the activity. In his quietness, he had soaked up the routines and rituals of a political convention that George had described, and he joined in the ruckus. Clearly engaged, he argued for his position and loudly cheered for his professed candidate. Only the unusual spelling (or misspelling) on his sign hinted that he was a special education student.

Adam swung into action again in the next unit. A week after the convention, students were debating affirmative action. George had assigned them texts to read that presented opposing views. He had given them a Venn diagram to capture the similarities and differences in the arguments of the two texts. A few days later, students started to formally debate the topic. Again Adam was animated. When it was time for the class to end, Adam was not ready for the discussion to be over. Still talking to a classmate, Adam kept asking for evidence to support his classmate's position. "Gentlemen," George tried to interrupt, "you're going to be late for science. You've got to get going." Acknowledging his comment with a slight nod, the two of them slowly moved out of the room. Their debate could be heard as they moved down the hall to their next class.

At the end of the following hour, Ellen, the science teacher, met George in the hallway. "What in the world did you do in there? I couldn't get them focused on science. They just kept arguing about affirmative action."

This class—a class characterized by these teachers early in the year as *lethargic, unmotivated,* and *disinterested*—was engaged and energized by topics of interest and by a sense of informed opinion. Their reading, their attention in class, their deep thinking, and their perception that their opinions mattered had animated them—not only in the classroom, but beyond it into other parts of the school and, we're willing to bet, their lives outside of school.

Why Did Adam Succeed?

Unfortunately high schools are filled with students like Adam who struggle with learning disabilities and reach high school keenly unmotivated to learn. A curriculum designed to fill in the gaps by teaching them once again the basic skills is not going to work for them. Adam's history resounded with instances of underlining the nouns and verbs, of practicing the short *a* sound, and of writing formulaic paragraphs. He knew what it was like to fill pages of workbooks and to complete mind-dulling worksheets. "Boring," Adam said. "School is boring." When asked what was different in Mr. Marsh's class, he paused before he answered. "It's hard and it's fun. He makes us think." George had added the important element of challenge to Adam's experiences, and it had worked.

Education pundits often urge teachers to add rigor or challenge to the work they assign students; however, teachers talk about being confused about what that means. Does it mean assigning more work? Asking students to complete more complex projects? What exactly does rigor mean? How do we increase challenge? We need to give meaning to these terms by identifying specific steps, because that rigor, that challenge, made all the difference for Adam and his classmates.

▶ *The Role of Argument*

George's approach was to structure his curriculum around argument. He knew that there were facts students needed to learn, but he embedded them within interesting problems that students could wrestle with and that had no easy answers: problems that were arguable and required critical reasoning. Mike Schmoker, in *Results Now* (2006), stresses the value of bringing argument into the classroom: "Children in the earliest grades will argue with force and passion, will marshal evidence, and will employ subtlety on behalf of their favorite athletes, pop stars, and automobiles. This is the mind—the intellect—in action" (68). Dates, names, and other historical facts, Schmoker contends, are meaningless until they are framed into arguments that can fully engage learners. This, he argues, is the essence of education that ushers students into a democracy in action. Exciting, energizing, and action filled, the curriculum with argument at its center is what hooks learners, including those like Adam.

It was in this rich environment that Adam was willing to hone his reading and writing skills. Here he used nouns and verbs to argue a point instead of just identifying and underlining them. His skills grew as he needed them, just as Stevi became a better skier by stretching her skills on more difficult slopes.

Moreover, Adam was being educated by doing what educated people do: think critically about issues, develop arguments, and engage in ongoing debate about important issues. Adam read articles that his teachers knew would challenge him because he was curious about the topics at hand and because he wanted to be a full participant. And why is this important, especially for the adolescent? Ask any teacher and he'll tell you how often students ask, "Why are we doing this? What good is this?" If students don't see the work they're being asked to do mirrored in the world outside of school, they're not as willing to play the school game. Talk about a way to decrease motivation.

Look at the connection between the academic tasks George asked of his students and life outside of school. Students can turn on the television to see a political convention under way. Many students come from homes where parents engage in political discussions around the kitchen table. If nothing else, students can turn on the radio and hear talk shows discussing political issues. The work George asked of his students was familiar, not just school-book stuff. What students see outside of school often requires critical reasoning and, as a result, learning grounded in this dimension feels more real to students than work that requires memorization or lower-order skills.

▶ The Importance of Simulations

George's convention is an example of a simulation. Simulations are just what the name implies: a replication of an event that occurs in the world outside of school. Mock trials and weddings are just a few examples of simulations found in schools.

Anytime students role-play a situation that reflects real-world activities, they are involved in a simulation.

Simulations challenge students to think at a critical reasoning level. When well structured, simulations require students to transform their learning into a new form while adopting the perspective of someone else. Think of the nature of adolescents: egocentric and self-centered. Simulations offer an imaginary scenario where they envision and articulate the perspectives of others—even those with whom they completely disagree. By their very nature, simulations challenge students to move beyond their own perspectives and to consider those of others.

While this kind of thinking is hard, it's also fun. As Wilhelm and Smith (2006) point out, getting students involved through drama is highly motivating. Most students like the kind of thinking that goes into transforming their learning into an imaginary sequence. The shift from sitting passively at a desk to moving around the room portraying their understanding of concepts can alter the nature of the learning context from one that is stifling to one filled with energy . . . and deep learning.

▶ The Role of Questions

George was a master at asking questions. Too often teachers ask only questions that they know the answer to. (Stevi saw this only recently when she visited the classrooms of ten teachers over the space of two days. Not once did she hear teachers ask a question to which they didn't already have the answer.) George's questions pushed students to think in new ways about topics under discussion. Often his questions required students to think critically: What would lead someone to believe this way about an issue? What would it look like if a candidate didn't campaign negatively? What's another way of looking at this?

And instead of expecting quick answers, he frequently provided time for students to think about their answers. Sometimes he would ask them to write on the topic while other times he would ask students to think with a partner. After someone answered, he looked for other ways of viewing the same answer, frequently asking for another viewpoint.

At the same time, he taught students how to ask questions. He talked about different levels of questions: factual recall questions with right or wrong answers, inferential questions that required students to connect their background knowledge with the text that they were reading, and experiential questions that pulled from students' backgrounds. As a regular practice, he would provide time for students to generate questions and identify in small groups the questions they wanted to talk about. He found that not only were the students more willing to participate in discussions this way, but they frequently asked tough questions that challenged the thinking of all in the room.

▶ *The Imperative to Scaffold High Expectations*

On top of putting thinking at the center of his work with students, George held high expectations for all students, even those like Adam who had little history of academic success. He was a "warm demander" (Gay 2000). "It just takes scaffolding," George argued. "Some students need more support than others, but they will participate in my class. No ands, ifs, or buts about it." As we learned from Csikszentmihalyi, Adam needed to have the appropriate skills to meet the challenge. George knew that as he held expectations high, he must provide scaffolds that would lead to success. Without them, he was dooming Adam and other students to failure.

He provided multiple scaffolds, including modeling the kind of thinking Adam could do, putting Adam into supportive groups, using graphic organizers to structure his thinking, and nudging him to think further about the topics under study. This was the scaffolding that George argued is so important. (See Figure 6–1 for more tips about scaffolding.)

George modeled the kinds of activities that might occur at a political convention and coached his students by asking probing questions (and explaining his reasons for asking them), encouraging them to think and rethink positions. As students read articles, George revealed his own thinking process while reading. He showed them how he questioned the evidence and wondered about the credentials of the writer. Instruction about how to develop an effective argument was embedded into the daily lessons, just as was instruction in how to form an effective response to the content. For each requirement of the final assessment, George created a packet of graphic organizers to help each learner clearly understand how to be successful. Students had the context, and George showed them directly how to think deeply about the issues under study.

Along with providing the scaffolding in terms of instruction, George pulled in people resources. Knowing that Adam would need more support than other students, George worked with Adam's resource teacher, who often visited the class. She was not present just for Adam, however. Instead, she worked with all of the students so that Adam's cognitive needs were not made public. By planning with George and spending time in class, she knew what was expected and was able to provide additional support to Adam during their resource time.

After the classroom political convention, students continued discussing issues for weeks. On the night of the actual election, 220 students, parents, and

Tips for Scaffolding Challenging Tasks

1. The teacher needs to know students' skills, knowledge, and strategies that will lead them to be successful. *Checking in and checking out* are necessary in order for the teacher to know how much scaffolding to put into place.
2. Use the least amount of scaffolding necessary for student success.
3. Keep in mind the end goal: students independently accomplishing rigorous work. Provide enough scaffolding for success and remove that scaffolding when students no longer need it.
4. The teacher needs a repertoire of scaffolds, which might include the following:
    - modeling
    - asking probing questions
    - providing specific feedback
    - thinking aloud
    - collaborative learning
    - creating need-based groups that are led by the teacher
    - providing graphic organizers
    - providing instruction on thinking strategies
5. The teacher needs to create social contexts for students to interact together and solve problems *collaboratively*. In groups, students need to occasionally work as the most capable member as well as receive assistance from their peers.

Figure 6–1 *Tips for Scaffolding Challenging Tasks*

family members attended an evening seminar at the high school. Democrats, Republicans, and Independents met in small groups throughout the high school classrooms to watch the results of the election and to continue their discussions of the issues.

Believing in Possibilities

> In a study by Wentzel (2002) students' perceptions of their teachers' expectations for their learning was a strong predictor of how responsibly they engaged in their academic work, how helpful they were to classmates, how interested they were in class, and how much they desired to learn. (National Research Council 2004, 45)

Ensuring that curriculum is challenging for all students is grounded in a teacher's belief system. If a teacher does not believe that her students can do tough work even with support, it is unlikely that she will offer them appropriately challenging work. On the other hand, a teacher who believes that students just need to toughen up and reach the challenges is also unlikely to provide the appropriate scaffolding or assistance. There's a balance here. For teachers to hold those important high expectations, they need to provide adequate support for student success. Scaffolding does matter, if we do indeed believe that all students can learn.

For More Information

To learn more about challenge, here are three books and a couple of websites you might find of interest.

▶ Books

Keene, E. 2008. *To Understand: New Horizons in Reading Comprehension*. Portsmouth, NH: Heinemann.

National Research Council. 2004. *Engaging Schools*. Washington D.C.: National Academy Press

Wilhelm, J. 2002. *Action Strategies for Deepening Comprehension*. Jefferson City, MO: Scholastic.

———. 2007. *Engaging Readers and Writers with Inquiry*. New York: Scholastic.

▶ Websites

Critical Thinking Community (www.criticalthinking.org/): The Center for Critical Thinking is based on the work of Dr. Richard Paul, who is considered to be one of the early pioneers of modern critical thinking. This site contains information about critical thinking, teaching ideas, and research.

University of Delaware Problem Based Learning (http://www.udel.edu/pbl/). The University of Delaware site has information about problem-based learning as well as sample problems for the classroom.

7

Celebration

The Poetry Slam

The auditorium was filled with the energy of the teenagers setting the stage to look like a coffeehouse. Students played with the lights to get the right ambience while others adjusted the mics. A small group of students arranged their homemade backdrops, adding to the coffeehouse illusion.

In a classroom not too far away another group of students was rearranging the classroom: moving the desks into a horseshoe shape, setting up a microphone in the front of the room, dimming the lights, and playing soft jazz from a corner in the room.

"What about candles? Can we use them?" hollered a girl with spiky hair.

"Think of the fire code," Marne Gulley, the teacher, answered as she sat at her desk watching the students create the atmosphere they wanted for the next hour's performance.

Marne had arrived to school earlier than usual that day. Loving her job, she was known as one of the regular early birds, but today she was earlier than most days. No, she wasn't the play director, nor was she the drama teacher. Instead, she taught English to sophomores, and this morning crews from each class were preparing for their celebrations that were occurring throughout the day.

When Marne and her student teacher, Shereen AbuSaeed, first planned their poetry unit, they had no idea how invested students would become in preparing for the celebration: a poetry slam that, like an author's reception, would unveil the book of poetry each class would publish. The catch was that the students would be in charge. Marne and Shereen would be their cheerleaders, but they wouldn't be the organizers, nor would they prod. Instead, this would be the students' project. *They* would be in charge.

Each class decided on the committees it needed and assigned roles. An editing committee oversaw the publication and the work of the other committees, including word processors and illustrators. Some students volunteered to be the crews to design and set up the celebration itself. One of the more outgoing students in each class was the emcee. The one standard requirement was that all students had to author a poem that the editorial board thought was of high enough quality to be included in the class anthology.

On the day of the slam, the program committees handed out their programs, clearly proud of their work. The emcees took the stage and introduced each performer. The poems ranged from serious, dark poetry to the light and nonsensical. When the first poets took to the stage, it hadn't taken long for the audience members to get into the mood. They snapped their fingers in rhythm to some of the poems, stood up and cheered at the end of others, and nodded in sympathy to the sad ones.

After the slam, students gathered around the food that the refreshment committee had brought. Students relived the performances, commenting about the emotional experience that they had just shared together. Even though each class had the same assignment—publish a class poetry book and present it at the slam—each one was unique. Marne and Shereen had guided, nudged, and taught them the skills needed for success, but the students did the work and in the end celebrated the results of their efforts.

At the end of the day, Marne and Shereen should have been exhausted, but instead they were energized. "I haven't seen this group of students so engaged in their work. Everyone turned in a poem. Everyone! Can you believe it?" Marne exclaimed. In this school where many students saw little hope for their future, rarely was such engagement evident.

No wonder the teachers were so energized at the end of the day.

Why Take the Time?

When there is reason to think that we are appreciated, job satisfaction is usually high: whereas the greatest source of stress in the workplace is the feeling that no one is interested in supporting our goals. (Csikszentmihalyi 1990, 113)

Frequently, teachers talk about how they used to have time for fun such as celebrations and activities like poetry slams. State assessments, adequate yearly progress, and NCLB changed that. Taking time out of a full curriculum to celebrate, such as what Marne and Shereen did, must have a clear payoff in order for teachers to invest the time needed to plan and take time away from the academics.

And it is worth the time! Celebrating student accomplishments on a regular basis is key to motivation and engagement. Letting students know their work and efforts are recognized, honored, and appreciated can motivate them to exert the kind of effort necessary to improve scholastically, socially, and emotionally. Building days to celebrate throughout a unit creates a culture that expects success from all students. As the famous quote by Thomas J. Peters reminds us, "Celebrate what you want to see more of."

Think of celebration as a public ritual that recognizes students' efforts. Other rituals fill the school year: pep rallies, award assemblies, graduations, birthday parties, proms, and homecoming games. Families often celebrate birthdays, anniversaries, and small moments like chores completed without reminders. Adult lives are filled with events that are ritual-like: bachelor parties, baptisms, Fourth of July picnics. Many corporations mark special events with formal celebrations: holiday parties, awards for distinguished employees, retirement parties. Each of these celebrations commemorates an accomplishment or a memorable event, shining the spotlight on the moment, reminding a community of its shared tradition.

It's not uncommon for celebrations to be the occasions for stories that are told and retold: Uncle Sam's one drink too many, the chairman's outlandish flirtation with a secretary, the lost set of keys at the family reunion. In Stevi's family, part of the birthday celebration was going to a special movie that the birthday child wanted. To this day, she groans about all the awful John Wayne movies she had to see because of her brother's birthday movie choice while he reminds her that he had to sit through *The Sound of Music* and silly romances.

Celebrations in classrooms need to do the same: publicly affirm the importance of each individual in the community, loudly declare the accomplishments of students who form that classroom community, and provide the plot for stories that students tell over and over again. Regular celebrations let students know that the time and energy they put into the work are worthy of that effort, a component of intrinsic motivation. These celebrations also let them know that they matter.

Of course, the importance of publicly acknowledging good work is common sense, but other reasons, well grounded in research, attest to the importance of celebrating students if we care about motivation and engagement. In one study, researchers found that if schools are serious about improving motivation, they need to recognize student accomplishments daily. This study (and others) shows the obvious: students are willing to exert effort when their teachers show interest in their academic progress (Springs and Kritsonis 2008).

A clear way that celebrations—both spontaneous and planned ones—serve to nurture motivation and engagement is simply by generating fun. Even though students complained about being nervous performing at Marne and Shereen's poetry slam, they still had a tremendous amount of fun, and this element of fun is a motivator. After all, intrinsic motivation is built on the notion that students will continue doing the kinds of things they have fun doing (Newmann 1992).

Also, celebrations marry two powerful components for motivation and engagement: competence and connection (Ryan and Deci 2000). For celebrations such as Marne and Shereen's poetry slam, the work students produced in the slam itself and in the book revealed students' level of competence. There is no faking one's skill in writing poetry since the work is there for all to see. The bond between perception of competency and engagement is clear (Smith and Wilhelm 2006). Celebrations illuminate competence rather than flaws. By naming what students do well, teachers provide the scaffolding for developing an "I can do it" attitude, which leads to the self-efficacy necessary for engagement.

Because of their public nature, celebrations become part of the lore of the classroom, connecting the students through their shared experiences. For the rest of the school year, students in Marne and Shereen's classes talked about the poetry slam as an event unique to their community of learners. One class talked about how they transformed their classroom while the other laughed at their creative use of the huge auditorium. Another joked about the gaffe the emcee had made while others recalled dramatic moments during the slam. The poetry slam as well as other celebrations throughout the year became a thread that linked the students together. Celebrations as regular rituals build that sense of community that binds together a group and enhances the caring classroom community. (For more discussion of the importance of this type of classroom culture, see Chapter 2).

We know that celebration by itself is not necessarily an acknowledgment of student competence, but certain kinds of celebrations seem more likely to build a sense of efficacy: that "I can do it" belief in one's abilities. Celebrations that work for our purposes of nurturing motivation and engagement must be well grounded in authentic accomplishment. From the self-esteem era, we know the danger in celebrating mediocrity (Begley 2003b). Students discount praise for work that they know is inadequate. Celebrations must be about accomplishments: earnest, authentic accomplishments. Students need to have accomplished something that is meaningful, challenging, and substantive if celebration is to have the desired effect of motivating students and engaging them in future work.

Teacher Stance

Celebrating as the sixth C has implications for the teacher. It requires a particular stance or way of being that may run counter to what typically happens in schools. Often teachers watch their students carefully to understand misconceptions and to spot errors in thinking that need to be corrected. The stance that we're talking about, however, requires a teacher to value and search for strengths and sparks of insight. This calls for a commitment to look for reasons to celebrate and necessitates a teacher to develop routines and rituals that will make those celebrations happen.

▶ Being Vigilant

Consider that proverbial red pen. All too often teachers watch their students with a mental red pen ready to catch, document, and correct any possible error. With a vigilant eye searching for the mistake, the teacher hopes to eradicate the error by naming it. And too often—and with just slight exaggeration—the error overshadows the accomplishment. Teachers of writing too often note the glaring spelling error before they note the clever turn of a phrase. Teachers of history spot the error in dates before they note a student's attempt to think like a historian. Teachers of math look for the calculation error, only to miss an original way of solving a complex problem. But what would happen if teachers were as vigilant about looking for signs of brilliance as they are in finding the mistakes? What if teachers went on the hunt for strengths before spotting the deficiencies? What if we switched the deficiency model that too often reigns in classrooms to the asset model?

Teachers in classrooms designed to motivate and engage students need to put those metaphorical pens away—at least some of the time—and vigilantly look for student strengths. For the purposes of creating a culture in the classroom that nurtures motivation and engagement, the teacher's stance must shift from attention on the deficit to an urgent search for student strengths. Of course, we're not talking about glossing over errors. Instead, we're talking about having a healthy balance of praise and constructive criticism.

Marne reflected the kind of vigilance we're talking about. Even though it was 4:30 P.M. on a Thursday when we sat down to talk with her, she was excited, enthusiastic, and knowledgeable as she spoke about her methods to celebrate students. She talked about her experiences as a literacy coach. "I can walk into a classroom and tell if the teacher wants to be there. Those teachers know what students do well and are always on the hunt for that. If I can see this, think of what the students are thinking."

Stevi remembers a friend's advice from years ago. Judy Gilbert, former language arts consultant at the Colorado Department of Education, would urge teachers to look for what they could see in their students rather than what was missing. If we look for what they can do, Judy would explain, we can name it for them and then celebrate it. If we look for what's missing, we begin our work with students with a focus on the deficit, which discourages rather than motivates.

This stance is terrifically important. Stevi often uses an article by Sharon Begley (2003a), a former science columnist for the *Wall Street Journal*, to illustrate this point in workshops. Begley explains recent studies on the Pygmalion effect: Expect to see good, and you'll see it. Expect to see problems, and you'll see them. In one study mentioned in the article, the experimenter's attitude toward rats even influenced how the experimenter trained the rats to run mazes. Twelve experimenters were given several rats to train. Six were told that their rats had the genetic make-up of geniuses while the other six were told they had rats known to be slow. Those "slow" rats finished the maze after the "smarter" rats. Of course, there was no such thing as a smarter species or a slower species. This experiment showed that expectations even for rats affected how they were trained and the results of that training.

Teachers are not lab scientists, and students aren't lab rats racing through a maze. However, these experiments reinforce the importance of a teacher's stance toward students. If teachers expect to find problems and search for deficiencies in student learning, they will find them, and students will be reminded of their flaws. However, if teachers see their students as capable and competent and seek evidence of their smartness, they are positioned to celebrate rather than to mourn.

▶ Seeing the Potential in All Students

John remembers clearly when he first became aware of the importance of vigilantly searching for students' capabilities and strengths. Erin, a student in his Great Books and Great Ideas class, had failed every English course in high school. Needless to say, she came into the class with a chip on her shoulder. John and his co-teacher, Karen, knew immediately that Erin would be a challenge, but they were impressed with her keen insights into literature. Intentionally and with great effort, they ignored that chip on her shoulder and nudged her to put forth her best effort. When she slacked off, they pushed some more, and when she participated, they cheered her efforts. Often they challenged Erin to explain her insights and pushed her to think even more deeply. Erin took to the bait and argued with them. Animated and fully participating in class after class, Erin earned her first A.

When the first-quarter midterm grades were due, John and Karen called for a student-parent conference to celebrate her progress. Erin and her parents were expecting the worst. John began the conference. "We are so pleased that Erin is in our class; she has an A." Erin began to cry. Her parents began to cry.

Erin kept repeating, "I can't have an A; that's not me."

But it was. John and Karen saw her potential, nudged her growth daily, and celebrated her success with her parents.

▶ Making Every Day a Day of Celebrating

Even small celebrations can heighten the chances of students being motivated and engaged. Consider how the following three teachers made time for everyday celebrations.

Mike Roblin, a social studies teacher in Northglenn, Colorado, knew that small, everyday celebrations mattered. Every day before class started, he would shake the hands of students as they entered the room and thank them for coming to class. Often he would start class with the same announcement: "This is your chance to get a great education; I need you in my class!" Mike's approach made students want to come to his class. When Mike died of leukemia, the high school auditorium was standing room only. Hundreds of current and former students attended his service to say their good-byes to a teacher who celebrated each individual student each day he or she came to class.

Karen Hartman was a teacher and instructional leader at Thornton High School in Colorado. Along with teaching Basic Skills, a class for students who struggled with literacy, she also taught one of the International Baccalaureate classes. Karen made sure that students in both classes celebrated regularly. She baked cakes for birthdays, lit candles, and had students sing to each other. On days after students had worked particularly hard, she celebrated their efforts by bringing in cupcakes for them to munch on while they continued working. "The only time we stopped working," Karen explained, "was when we sang 'Happy Birthday.' But those small celebrations yielded results. My students—all of them—were willing to put their hearts and souls in the work because they knew how valued their efforts were. You've no idea how much I got out of them as a result of a little baking."

Remember Marne, whose poetry slam story introduced this chapter? Like Karen and Mike, Marne didn't save celebrations for the end of the unit only. Instead, Marne would send her students birthday cards, publicly announce student accomplishments in faculty meetings, and make sure that for every phone call home about a problem, she also made a positive call. What was the result of this work? On most days Marne's students came to class with a great attitude and were motivated and engaged. This was not usual in the school. At a school with more than two-thirds of the students on free and reduced lunch, many teachers voiced concerns about students' attitudes.

But not Marne.

▶ Going Public with Celebrations

Walk into most elementary schools and you'll find celebrations of students' accomplishments on classroom walls and even on hallway walls. Bulletin boards are filled with student work as well as mementos from students' lives. It's not uncommon to see photos of students and their families on those bulletin boards or digital photos that teachers have taken throughout the school year. Secondary teachers could learn from their elementary colleagues.

David Singer knows how to do this. He fills his room with student work. Every space of wall up to and sometimes including the ceiling includes student work from the beginning of the year until the present. After each class, he provides the students with sticky notes and tells them to write what they learned or what questions they have about the content. They paste these exit notes on the wall as they leave the room. Each day students know David cares about their understanding and celebrates their thinking.

At Montbello High School, former principal Antwan Wilson knew the importance of creating a culture that celebrates academic success. As students walked down a ramp to the classrooms, they viewed a wall that celebrated students who had been accepted into college. Photo after photo of seniors headed to college lined the walls, and each week the number grew.

▶ Keeping Track

For many years, Stevi was the codirector of the Colorado Writing Project. Each time the project addressed the topic of grading, she and other CWP consultants set the participants up. The day before the grading discussion, they collected a writing assignment from participants; that night they marked it up, looking only for errors (and occasionally making up the errors) and marking them harshly with their red pens. Then they randomly assigned letter grades to the writing. Only one paper "earned" an A while the other papers received random grades of B, C, D, and F. When Stevi handed back the "graded" papers, she made a big deal about the one and only A. Quickly the teachers looked at their neighbor's paper to see who had earned that single A. The moment the A was spotted, the teachers started jokingly mocking the writer.

"Teacher's pet."

"Kiss-up."

Even though the teachers by this time knew that they had been set up, they still joshed and teased the one whose paper had that shining A on it.

These teachers are no different from our students. If students see one or two people earning the high marks, they can be merciless to their peers. It's for this reason that teachers should be vigilant not only in their search for strengths but in looking for strengths in *all* students, from the academically gifted to the struggling students. To be certain that you are having positive interactions with all students, we urge you to keep track of intentional celebrations, whether they are large or small. John developed a checklist (see Figure 7–1) that he used both in his high school classroom and with his teacher candidates in his university classes. The list reminds teachers to continually celebrate students in a variety of ways.

Ways to Celebrate

There are many ways to celebrate, ranging from elaborate events, such as a poetry slam similar to Marne and Shereen's, described at the start of the chapter, to simple activities, such as Martha's Café. Martha McFarland, a teacher in Commerce City, Colorado, invites students at the end of each writing unit to share an excerpt from the work they've just completed. The students can read the entire piece or just a section of it. It doesn't matter, but what does matter is that each student shares and the class applauds.

Some of the following celebrations are simple, requiring little energy, while others call for substantial planning and effort. But as each teacher we talked to will attest, even the time-demanding celebrations are well worth the effort when teachers are deliberate at creating a climate marked by motivation and engagement.

▶ A Phone Call Home

A simple means of celebrating students' accomplishments is by making positive phone calls home. The results reveal that the few minutes it takes to make these phone calls are well spent. Both of us used this strategy to motivate our students and to earnestly congratulate them for work well done. When Stevi team taught, she and her partner agreed that as soon as they saw positive behavior from their freshmen, one of them would call home immediately. Often parents were working, so they would leave a message on the voice mail. All it took was a couple of minutes, and students, as well as parents, responding positively.

Celebration Checklist

Student Name	Phone Calls	Postcards	Bulletin Board	Email	Lunch Meetings	Individual Conferences	Parent Conferences	Other

Figure 7–1 *Celebration Checklist*

May be copied for classroom use. © 2009 by John McDermott and Stevi Quate, from Clock Watchers *(Heinemann: Portsmouth, NH).*

Teaching his ninety sophomores, John developed a plan where he would call one-third of his students' families every two weeks during the first quarter. These calls, brief and straight to the point, delivered a positive message to parents concerning their child's progress or behavior in class. Often parents would tell John, "Are you sure? This is the first positive call I have ever received from anyone at the schools. Thank you!"

After the first set of calls, John often heard conversations between students that went something like this:

Student 1: He called my house last night.

Student 2: Are you in trouble?

Student 1: No, he told my mom that I worked well at the end of class yesterday.

Student 2: What? He didn't call my home!

Student 2: Hey, McD, why didn't you call my home?

We knew that by being vigilant in searching for and acknowledging strengths, we encouraged the kind of behavior that we wanted from all students. A phone call home, even a call home to the parent of a teenager, was one way of celebrating what students were capable of doing.

▶ *Success Analysis Protocol*

Teachers at Horizon High, like teachers in many other schools, studied the art and craft of teaching in professional learning communities. As the coach of a Critical Friends Group (CFG), a type of professional learning community, Stevi often facilitated discussions structured around protocols, or specific ways of conversing, for teachers to examine student work, professional practices, and teacher dilemmas. The Success Analysis Protocol is one such protocol. Knowing it worked well with teachers, Stevi tried it out with her students. Each time she used it with students she was impressed with the results. Stevi and her colleagues learned that the Success Analysis Protocol was a powerful way of learning about students and of acknowledging a side of them that became fodder for celebrations.

The steps of the Success Analysis protocol for students are fairly simple:

1. The day before using the protocol, ask students to write a reflection about a time when they were successful in the content area. A success simply means that the results of what the students did exceeded their expectations or the expectations of others. For instance, a math teacher might ask students to

write about a time when they were successful coming to understand a difficult math concept. An English teacher might ask students to write about a language arts project that they were proud of, or a science teacher could ask students to reflect on a success in a science fair or a lab.

2. Move students into groups of four or five.

3. Have one student begin by describing the success.

4. The other students then ask clarifying questions about the success so that they are certain they understand the details of the success.

5. After the clarifying questions have been answered, the student describing the success scoots her desk away from the group and the group analyzes her success. She listens to the discussion but does not participate in it. In their discussion, the group members identify the elements that went into her success. They might talk about the amount of time she invested, the creativity, the support she needed, or any other element that made this situation something out of the ordinary. One student works as a scribe, jotting down all of the identified elements.

6. After the analysis, the second person describes his successful event. The rest of the group asks clarifying questions, and then they analyze that event, again with the scribe jotting down notes.

7. Once the group has analyzed everyone's success, the students' task is to compile a list of commonalities from each of their analyses. They could create a poster to hang in the room as an ongoing reminder of what it takes to be successful.

This protocol is a great way to acknowledge the successes students have had as well as to name the qualities that go into a success.

▶ An Auction as a Mini-Celebration

While teaching math, John arranged his students in coaching groups of four students for the duration of a unit of study. John explained, "For every personal goal and math objective you achieve during this two-week unit, you will receive a poker chip."

"Why, what are they good for?" one of the students asked.

"I won't let you know until the end of the unit, you want to make sure your group has garnered as many of these chips as possible," John encouraged.

"We gonna play poker?" a girl asked.

John replied, "No, but in a way you will be purchasing items important to your learning."

Each home group had its own plastic bag to hold the chips earned during the two-week period. John did his best to ensure a reasonably similar number of chips were in each bag. He awarded the chips for specific behavior such as completing a graphic organizer, participating in a seminar, helping others solve a challenging problem, or handing in homework.

When the unit was completed, John showed up at class with a brown bag filled with a variety of items. He announced, "Today we are going to have an auction. Each group has earned a number of chips during this unit. You will bid on the item in the paper bag without knowing the contents. This is a math lesson, so it is important to know there are fifteen items up for bid; some may be more appealing than others. You can only bid the number of chips you earned. Good luck."

Other norms for the bidding included the following:

- The teacher would accept the first bid heard from the group, so group members had to talk to each other and plan in advance.

- Groups would get the warning of "Going once, twice, sold" prior to completing a transaction.

- The teacher would remind students that there were fifteen items, so they would be wise to use their knowledge of probability and estimation to determine a plan for bidding.

Students began to arrange their chips in groups so they could be ready to bid. Students cheered when the item was of value and groaned loudly when the item was "lame" (see Figure 7–2). What's important to note is that the payoff for this activity was not during the initial event. When the next unit began, the chips took on more significance. Students became interested in how to earn chips for the next auction. The entire celebration took twenty minutes, but the effect on student engagement and building the classroom community lasted deep into the year.

▶ Heritage Day

During the Diversity unit at Horizon High School, we and the other American Studies Program teachers would host a Heritage Day. Students were told to clear off their dressers, bring pictures from their walls, and invite their family members to class to celebrate who they were. The teachers offered students a list of items for the big day.

Suggested Auction Items

One study session for the group with the teacher at a time of your choosing

A bag of chocolates

4 calculators

4 bookmarks listing the equations for volume of different shapes

A positive phone call home for each group member within the next week

4 Rubik's cubes

4 sets of notes for solving systems of equations

A set of pencils

A bag of potato chips

A six-pack of cola

4 pictures of the class taken earlier in the year

A set of gel pens

4 sets of stickers with positive statements (cool, you rock, awesome, etc.)

4 passes stating, "Get out of homework free"

Figure 7–2 *Suggested Auction Items*

The list included family pictures, favorite music (they could play one song as long as it was appropriate for the classroom), favorite food item, honors, awards, or recognitions they received, favorite book, favorite artwork, and any other items they could fit in a medium-sized box.

The day was a celebration of diversity. One young man brought his grandmother to class with a large bowl of the "best green chili." A young woman serenaded everyone with her violin. A student brought letters from the United States Civil War, handwritten by his great-great-great uncle. A young woman from Russia brought her dad to talk about escaping from Communism. Within each of these stories was a celebration of the students in these classes. As you can imagine, the students loved this day.

▶ Children's Book Celebration

At the end of each major unit, Karen Hartman made sure that her students celebrated their hard work together. For the culmination of writing units, she often had students read their work aloud with great fanfare, applause, and cookies. At the end of a letter-writing unit, she presented students with personalized stationery she had made on the computer, envelopes, stamps, more cookies, and soda. But her favorite celebration was toward the end of the year in her Basic Skills class.

For several weeks her students, all struggling readers, studied children's literature as preparation for their Friday visit to the nearby elementary school to read with their reading buddies. Karen still smiles when she thinks of the large, tough-looking guys squeezing into the small desks to read a book that they had practiced reading throughout the week. She often tells the story of one of her students in particular. Shyly sneaking in her room, he told his friends, who in turn told Karen, that he had ditched all his classes that day except for this one. He wanted to be there for his reading buddy.

One of the major tasks of this unit was for her students to write a children's book for their reading buddy. When the books were written, illustrated, and bound, they invited the first graders to their room for a book reading and signing plus cookies and lemonade. Everyone had a great time, and the little kids eagerly took their books with them.

▶ Awards Ceremonies

At the end of each semester, John handed out awards to each of the students in his class. The awards represented actual accomplishments in the classroom. He called each student to the front of the room and presented him with his award. Each award was tied directly to class performance. Applause and compliments filled the classroom.

▶ Celebration of Learning

It was the final week of the semester, and as students prepared for their culminating project, they were mentally exhausted. For the project, they had to summarize their learning from the semester in a format of their choosing. Students had to identify a theme for the summary and support the theme with concrete information learned in the previous months. After multiple student-teacher conferences, individual scaffolding, workshopping, and considerable self-assessment, students were in need of a break. This break was the Celebration of Learning.

The Celebration of Learning had been planned much earlier in the semester. John began bringing his video camera to school in order to capture memorable moments. When students made their Rube Goldberg projects, John was filming.

When they flew their bottle rockets to demonstrate principles of physics, the camera was rolling. When they wrote essays, participated in dramatic presentations, gave speeches, wrote songs about their content, played sports, conducted seminars, and walked in the hall between classes, John was capturing the students' lives on tape.

John took the multiple videos home, sat down at his computer with a moviemaking program, and went to work. He captured the most appealing portions of student work—making sure each student in the class was in the final film—and added music to the nine-minute video.

Within minutes during the showing of the tape, students were laughing, patting each other on the back, and making statements like "I remember that. It was really cool!" The timing could not have been better. With smiles on their faces, students were ready to return to the work of preparing for the culminating project.

This Is Your Celebration

A few years ago, Stevi, along with Karen Hartman and Sheila Kaehny, worked with teachers in a township outside of Dundee, South Africa. Each day of the two-week workshop began with the South African teachers singing together. Standing in a circle, they listened to the teachers begin one song and then continue with another. Together they swayed with the music and laughed as one teacher after another broke into a dance. Each day began with this ritual that celebrated another day of being able to work and learn together. Often Stevi thinks about the way the songs and the dances helped build their learning community and how this communal act set them all up for the day. For the fifteen minutes of being together in song and dance, the payoff was tremendous: the day began with a heightened sense of motivation and a willingness to engage.

Imagine what would happen if a regular part of the school day included time for such celebrations.

Imagine starting the day with Kool and the Gang's song, "Celebration."

8

Putting It All Together
The Six Cs as a Braided River

A few years ago, Stevi stood on the banks of a gray, cold, fierce river in the small town of Talkeetna, Alaska. The river was long and wide and full of energy. Stepping back a bit, she could see that the massive river contained a myriad of channels, smaller rivers that braided themselves together to form this large mass. These smaller rivers, at one time gentle and slow, had meandered down from the glaciers, eventually merging with others; now braided together, they had transformed into a large, wild river, full of vigor. Without the separate rivers, the larger river would not exist, but as they joined together, they formed a new kind of force.

The six Cs are similar to those braided rivers. Each C, a separate entity like the smaller rivers, can stand alone and do the work it needs to do; however, when united with the other Cs, the result is a mighty force like that river in Talkeetna. A classroom in which students are motivated and engaged is energetic and forceful, while a classroom with only one or two of the Cs in place may be a grand place to learn, but it will lack the strength, the *velocity*, if you will, of a powerful river after the smaller rivers have merged. When we talk about the motivation and engagement framework, we talk about each of the Cs separately, but we know it's the velocity of the large river that we want: it's the braiding of all six Cs that leads to classrooms where students are motivated to learn and remain engaged in the process.

When we explained our metaphor of braided rivers to an artist friend, Shaun Armour, Shaun talked about the image that he visualized. What a surprise it was to see his image come to life. (See Figure 8–1.)

The Evolution of Practice

Lou Ann Nelsen and Steve Lash learned the importance of intentionally braiding together each of the six Cs. Lou Ann, a social studies teacher, and Steve, an English teacher, were teaching partners in American Studies, a sophomore interdisciplinary course. For two hours each day, they taught forty-nine students a curriculum that integrated English and social studies. Strong, experienced teachers, they had nodded in agreement with each of the six Cs as they studied them. "Isn't it what good teachers do intuitively?" they asked.

After all, they recognized the importance of creating that caring classroom culture and were certain they had done that. They knew that they needed to check in on their students' learning and check out their progress during each of their units. But only infrequently did they create a pre-assessment that mirrored the post-assessment, and only once in a while did they include students in the

Figure 8–1 *Braided River—Artwork by Shaun Armour*

assessment process. They incorporated group work and choice now and then. Challenge was a strength—perhaps too much so, since nearly a third of their students were failing, leaving them little to celebrate. Despite Lou Ann and Steve's intentions to weave all the six Cs into their instruction, their students were still unmotivated and disengaged.

"Our sophomores are wonderful people; we love them. But they just cannot seem to get focused enough to succeed in our class," Lou Ann explained.

"We've tried everything. We even held voluntary after-school study groups, but things haven't improved," Steve added. "Attendance is generally good and these are the nicest bunch of students you ever want to meet. We are willing to try anything to improve their learning."

"Our low performers are not into school and our higher-performing students are getting irritated. Group work is not very productive. Over spring break they are doing the post-Depression photo story based on historical data. They are supposed to be working in pairs; however, most wanted to simply work alone even though the class is highly social."

"A big problem," Steve added, "is that we don't have many strong leaders. On top of that, our students just aren't motivated to learn."

Even though it was April and the year was winding down, Lou Ann and Steve wondered what would happen if they were conscientious about including the six Cs in their planning of the last unit of the year. Knowing that motivation and engagement were at the base of their students' learning problems, they wanted to end the year on a high note. Of course, we wouldn't be telling their story if their students hadn't succeeded. At the end of the unit, forty-three out of forty-nine students handed in their final papers. By itself, this was a success story, but better yet, the class average on the assessment was a B. What happened in this class to allow for this increase in learning?

We want to tell the story of how Lou Ann and Steve braided the six Cs together and the difference this braiding made for their students. Even though we describe each of the Cs separately, you'll notice that many of the instructional strategies could fit into other categories. Think of them as separate channels merging to form a larger force.

The Rivers Intertwine

▶ The Caring Classroom Community

Nearly every indication possible pointed to the fact that this was a caring classroom community. Lou Ann and Steve knew their students and greeted them warmly as they walked in the room. The students were pleasant in their interactions with their friends and their teachers. However, as Lou Ann and Steve began paying close attention to how students interacted with each other, they realized that the community appeared strong when the focus was on teacher-student interactions. They were most surprised when they began paying close attention to student-student interactions. They noticed who was sitting with whom and how frequently students would point to someone on the other side of the room instead of calling the person by name. Out of curiosity, they began checking to see if the students knew each other, and to their chagrin, the classmates didn't. Sure, students who sat in close proximity to each other knew each other's names, and students who spent time together in other classes knew each other, but a surprisingly large number of students were still unsure of names of people who had shared their class for more than six months.

Realizing that the classroom community was strong between teachers and students but not between students and students, Lou Ann and Steve set out to build a stronger community, even though it was relatively late in the year. As they planned the year's final unit, they built in objectives that ensured students would get to know others in the class. A look at one class period shows how their plans played out.

It was about a week into the unit. Right before the bell rang, two girls wandered into the room, fully engaged in a conversation about their weekend plans. In the back corner of the room, three boys, all in sports jerseys, were deep in a conversation about the evening's game. Steve and Lou Ann greeted the students as they walked in, often asking questions about their personal lives.

"How's it going?" Steve asked a tall sophomore. "Did you get your car running?"

"Sure thing, dude. It was just something simple." He sprawled in his seat, dropping his backpack loudly on the floor next to him.

As the bell sounded, Lou Ann finished writing the essential question and goals for the day on the whiteboard. One goal stated: "Students can write the first and last name of ten students in the classroom."

Steve announced to the students, "OK, take out a sheet of paper for the name quiz. Mrs. Nelsen and I will tap ten of you on the shoulder and you will come up to the front of the room and be stared at." Many of the students laughed. Steve numbered off the students from one to ten. "Please write their names." The students began to write quietly. When the results were recorded, 90 percent of the students could name all ten students correctly.

Not surprised that the students did so well, Lou Ann and Steve recognized that their efforts at building the classroom community were paying off. Convinced that all of the instruction had to be grounded within their content, they had figured out academic ways to ensure that students knew each other. Following are some of the activities they used.

Paseo[1]

Early in the unit, Steve and Lou Ann cleared all the desks out of the center of the room. They then divided the students into halves. They asked half of the students to stand in a large circle. The other half then had to move into the center of the circle, find a partner, and stand facing this person. The instructions were simple:

- Those in the inside and the outside circle alternated between being a speaker and a listener based on which role the teacher assigned the two circles.

- For each round, the teacher posed a question for the speaker to address.

- While the speaker responded to the question, the listener listened only and did not speak. However, the listener was instructed to provide nonverbal signals that she was listening, so nodding, smiling, and gesturing for more information were encouraged.

- After about two minutes, the roles were switched so that the speaker became the listener while the listener was the speaker.

- At the end of the round, the teacher moved the students in one of the circles so that each student had a new partner. For instance, the teacher might say, "Inside circle, move three people to your right."

- This process of speaking, listening, and moving to a new partner continued until all of the questions had been answered or the teacher determined that the time was up.

Each time the students met a new partner, Lou Ann and Steve asked students to introduce themselves, even if they were partners with their best friend or someone they'd known since kindergarten.

The questions they posed to the speakers all focused on the content:

- What do you know about the beginning of World War II?

- What causes war?

- How do people end wars?

---

1. Thanks to the National School Reform Faculty (www.nsrfharmony.org/) for this process. Even though it was intended to be used with teachers, Lou Ann and Steve slightly altered the process to use it with their students.

- What would you do if you had to fight in a war?

- How can war be just?

The Paseo became one of many strategies the teachers used to strengthen the classroom community while students were learning the content.

Trios

Like Paseo, Trios requires students to interact with others whom they typically don't work with. First the teacher directed students to find two people they hadn't talked to that day and introduce themselves. They then gave the trios a topic to talk about. For instance, the first prompt was to talk about how Hitler came to power.

After about three minutes, the teacher directed students to find two new people whom they had not yet talked to that day. After introductions, the students responded to the new discussion prompt. This process continued for another two or three rounds so that by the end of the activity, students had talked to eight to ten unfamiliar students.

Card Passing

The teachers used Card Passing as a means to help students learn the vocabulary for this unit. It required movement as well as interaction with their classmates. As students entered the room, Steve handed them each a card with a vocabulary word on it. Once the bell rang, Lou Ann turned on the DVD player and catchy music filled the room. Students stood up and moved around the room, exchanging cards. When the music stopped, students partnered up with the last person they had exchanged cards with. After stating each other's first and last names, they worked at defining their word to their partner. They did this as quickly as possible with the goal of defining each word before the music started up again. The music signaled that it was time to move around the room and exchange cards once again. This process continued for three or four rounds.

Four Heads Are Better Than One

Building community wasn't always serious. Steve and Lou Ann also made sure students laughed together. This was evident the day that Lou Ann and Steve used Four Heads Are Better Than One. (See Chapter 5 for details on how to set this up.) After encouraging students to review their notes over the social studies content, their vocabulary, and the literature, Lou Ann chose four names out of a hat and called those students to the front of the room. She explained the rules: "We will ask you a question and you four must answer in complete sentences. However, each of you may say only one word at a time; you cannot coach or share answers with each other. When one person decides that the answer is correct and the sentence is complete, that person says, 'Period.'"

Steve began by asking the four to use *vivid* in a sentence.

Standing in a straight row facing the rest of the class, the four students hesitantly constructed a sentence. Each stated one word, trying hard to build off the previous words. The rest of the class listened intently.

The first student began, "Sometimes . . ."

The second student added, "there . . ."

The third student quickly said, "are . . ."

The fourth student paused and then said, "vivid . . ."

The first student glanced at the fourth student, scrunched up her eyebrows, and added, "images . . ."

The second student said, "in . . ."

"a . . . ," added the third student.

The fourth student said, "child's . . ."

The first student smiled and said, "mind . . ."

"Period," added the second student as loud as she could.

The students in the class applauded and laughed. Lou Ann and Steve then called up another four students to answer the next review question. Within the laughter, the students—every one of them—seemed to be engaged during the thirty minutes that the quiz took. Students leaned in to listen hard to their friends in front of the room and whispered to each other the word they would have said had they been standing in the front.

Each of the activities served dual purposes: learning the content and building a classroom community. Lou Ann and Steve found that braiding these activities into content related work was invaluable for strengthening their classroom community and that resulted in enhanced student learning.

▶ Checking In, Checking Out

In their planning, Lou Ann and Steve thought long and hard about their outcomes and the assessment process. In the past, they had been casual with the process of planning backward, but for this unit, they were very intentional. They planned the postassessment and then determined how they would preassess. They worried about checking out the learning along the way, knowing that if they didn't carefully monitor students' understanding, they could lose them early on. To address this issue, they decided to give a folder to each student, instructing him to keep all notes, drafts, and journals in it; the folders would be left in the room. This way, Steve and Lou Ann could each grab a few at night and quickly check on student understanding.

On the first day of the unit, Lou Ann and Steve had students begin discussing the unit's essential question: How does war transform society? They then explained the outcome of the unit: Students would show their understanding of the essential question by writing a commentary that compared the United States' entry into World War II with our entry into the Iraq War. They showed the students the rubric that they would use to assess the commentary.

Lou Ann and Steve also announced that the students were about to show off their current learning about the essential question. "True, you may not know much about how war transforms society at this moment, but we want to find out what you do know." They handed students a graphic organizer to help them plan their essay and encouraged them to write their thoughts on the subject.

After students had written their draft, Steve and Lou Ann distributed the folders. Each folder was labeled with the essential question and contained a copy of the commentary rubric. Lou Ann explained, "We put the rubric and all work in this folder and used it each day. We were very protective of these folders. They did not leave the classroom. As a result, there was no issue with a student claiming to leave his folder at home." At the end of the unit, two students thanked the teachers for requiring them to use the folders. Both had passed the unit and therefore the semester because of that simple organizational structure.

Throughout the entire unit, Lou Ann and Steve regularly checked the folders to see evidence of student understanding. For example, after a day of discussing the United States' entry into World War II, they asked students to answer this question: Based on the evidence, should the United States have entered World War II? That night, Lou Ann and Steve responded to each of the students' journals. Their brief responses focused exclusively on content. Because their goal was to check out students' understanding of content from their write-to-learn work, Lou Ann and Steve ignored misspellings, grammar, and other conventions. "We can fix those errors later when they do more formal writing," Steve explained. He knew that writing-to-learn activities, such as the journal writing, needed to focus on ideas over conventions.

▶ Celebration

Throughout the unit, Steve and Lou Ann ensured that they were celebrating student accomplishments. Of course, the culminating project, the commentary, provided a formal occasion to celebrate, but they didn't want to wait that long to publicly acknowledge students' good work. One of their most successful celebrations occurred early in the unit, right after the students had completed the pre-assessment: the draft of their commentary. That evening, Steve and Lou Ann hit the phones. They called parents to let them know how well their students had performed that day. When no one was home, they left a message on the answering machine with specific references to what the student had accomplished that day.

Lou Ann had wondered if the time spent phoning homes would be worth it, but the results amazed her. "When students came to class, the students started talking about it. They realized we called virtually everyone. They thought it was cool."

One student told Steve, "My parents don't believe you called. My grandmother answered the phone, and my parents don't believe her. Could you please call again?" Steve did, and he wrote a note to the parents as well.

The parental response surprised them, too. Many of the parents they talked to found it hard to believe they received a positive phone call. One parent called back the following day, leaving a message on Steve's voice mail. "We never get calls on my daughter. You don't know how important it is for parents of 'good kids' to hear from teachers! Please feel free to call anytime."

▶ Challenge

Steve and Lou Ann paid close attention to how they were challenging students while at the same time providing adequate support for student success. While making sure that students had plenty of opportunities to explore the essential question of the unit, they challenged students to think about war's impact on society through different lenses. Refusing to settle for easy answers, they had students visit and revisit ideas after examining different perspectives about the issues under study.

For instance, when students studied the impact of the Iraqi War on the United States, they were asked to grapple with the issue of whether or not we should have entered the war. Students watched a series of video clips that reflected varying points of view on the subject. They watched both a conservative view from a Fox News analyst and an analysis by a liberal group. They viewed clips that were obviously partisan and clips that claimed to be neutral. Students gathered the facts from each of the video clips, compared the perspectives, and wrestled with the reliability of sources. Their analysis became their ticket to participate in a seminar where they thoughtfully examined the facts they had gathered. At the conclusion of the seminar, students generalized their thinking by answering the question: When should the United States enter into a war?

What difference did this process make for motivation and engagement? Steve and Lou Ann were surprised at the impact. "This was a powerful process," Steve explained. "Many students didn't understand 9/11 and its impact on our country. After watching the video clips and seminaring about this topic, some of them became highly emotional. When I checked in with them, they told me that they hadn't understood what 9/11 was about, and the Iraqi War confused them. Now they understood both on an intellectual and an emotional level."

Throughout the school year, students had written numerous five-paragraph essays. For this assignment, however, Steve and Lou Ann abandoned the traditional format to see what would happen if they provided students with mentor texts—texts that modeled the kind of writing students were expected to do and that provided insights into ways that they might organize their writing and craft their ideas.

Steve and Lou Ann decided to use two commentary writers for mentors: Ernie Pyle, an award-winning columnist from World War II, and Leonard Pitts, a contemporary columnist with an award-winning column about September 11. After showing the class commentaries written by the two journalists, they guided students into an analysis of how the writers made their points. The students identified a variety of crafts the writers used: the "telling detail," the provocative story intended to illustrate a point, the snappy ending that left the reader thinking. They carefully examined the ways that the two writers organized their commentaries and fleshed out their theses, sometimes explicitly stated and other times implied. Steve explained to the students that they were to be a Leonard Pitts or an Ernie Pyle as they wrote their commentaries in response to the essential question.

One student asked, "You mean we aren't writing the five-paragraph essay?"

Steve answered, "Nope; you're writing a commentary in the style of Pyle or Pitts. We're going to revisit the rubric tomorrow so you'll know exactly what you have to do."

The student mumbled under his breath, "Darn! I'd rather write the five-paragraph essay. Now I have to think."

This comment struck Steve immediately. He began to wonder if the five-paragraph formula truncated the thinking students needed to do. Did the structure of the five paragraphs actually undercut the challenge and perhaps lead to disengagement?

He had a lot to think about.

▶ *Choice*

Super Saturday had always been a big day at Horizon High School. A tradition established when the school had opened, Super Saturday was a chance for the community to be involved in student presentations. Parents, friends, and community members were invited to learn from and with the students. Many Horizon teachers incorporated Super Saturday projects as an option in their curriculum. Since the school board's policy was that Super Saturday could not be a course requirement, participation was the result of personal choice, not an assignment.

Steve and Lou Ann invited students to participate in Super Saturday, urging them to invite their parents to join them in a seminar discussion on the question: How does war transform society? They organized students who chose to be a part of Super Saturday into collaborative teams. Each team of students knew they would be in charge of their seminar and could take the seminar in any direction they wanted.

According to Lou Ann and Steve, the results amazed them, especially considering that this was a group of students they had described as unmotivated and rarely engaged in their learning. "We asked students to volunteer to be group facilitators. They had to come and talk to us about why they wanted to facilitate and how they would organize the groups. Even one of our students who was eventually expelled was motivated to facilitate and did a great job," Lou Ann said, beaming.

Steve added, "We told them to dress nicely for the parents. We conducted workshops around the themes of fear and anticipation. We practiced facilitating seminars and discussed how to deal with parents who might want to dominate the seminar."

Lou Ann added, "Forty-three out of forty-nine students participated in this Saturday event. It was an incredible day. Some of the parents asked if we could do this again."

One parent even said, "I did not know this was going on in the world—thank you!" One of the groups continued long after the ending time for the seminar. The teachers, parents, and students were deeply engaged in the learning.

When Lou Ann and Steve approached this assignment through invitation by letting students choose whether or not they would spend a Saturday at school, students were not only motivated to do the work but also engaged in the process—and so were the parents.

▶ Collaboration

Group work was not new to Steve and Lou Ann. They often asked students to pair up or to jigsaw a reading. Like many teachers, they tended to move students randomly into groups or let students form groups on their own. For this unit, though, Steve and Lou Ann were more mindful about the setup of the groups, selecting group members for long-term coaching groups to work on projects and clarifying the reason for who should work together in short-term groups. Previously, they had assumed students had acquired the skills for working collaboratively, so only on occasion were they explicit about how to work with their peers. In this unit, however, they thought about the skills students would need to successfully complete group tasks.

Along with monitoring how students were collaborating, they were thoughtful about timing. For each collaborative task, they assessed how long it should take students to complete and then announced a slightly shorter deadline, thus exerting pressure for students to get on task and stay there. If students worked hard but still needed more time, they would often offer additional time; otherwise, they stuck with the original timing. Another trick to capture students' attention was to give them time limits stated in odd increments (12 minutes and 22 seconds) or complicated terms (323 seconds). This kept them pushing forward and pacing their progress.

All of this added up to highly productive group work; even the students who complained about working in groups at the start of the unit were ultimately satisfied with the results of the collaboration.

Flexible Groups

Lou Ann and Steve frequently moved students into short-term groups to work on a content-related task. Within these flexible groups, they taught students the skills needed to collaborate successfully. One lesson in the middle of the unit illustrates how they wove instruction on the skills for collaboration into the task.

The students were working on POWs (problems of the week), and Lou Ann and Steve hoped they would jigsaw their learning. Lou Ann announced the task: "We're going to follow up on the POW you've been working on this week. The first thing you'll do is meet with others who are studying the same issue you're studying. Those of you working on Warsaw will meet over here. Those studying the final solution, meet at the front of the room." She continued to assign areas of the room for the other POW topics. "Once in your groups, you'll have seven minutes and sixteen seconds to compare notes, making sure your notes are complete."

At the end of the time, Steve took over. "OK, let's do just what you've done in the past without the note-taking guide; find three people who worked on a topic other than yours. You have ninety seconds, so go!"

Once students were in new groups, Steve asked, "Can you see the face of everyone in your group?" He had talked quite a bit to the students about the importance of "looking like a group," which included being able to see everyone in the circle. "You're taking notes on your own note paper. You need to get started."

In one group, a student stepped into the leadership role. "Who has an A?"

"I do. I have Aryan race."

Lou Ann reminded the groups as they started speaking over each other, "Ladies and gentlemen, remember we have only one voice going at one time."

While the students shared the information, Lou Ann and Steve monitored the content of the discussion and the group processes. Because of this careful structuring of the work and an intriguing topic, students were engaged in the discussion.

Project-Based Coaching Groups

Several times during the unit, Lou Ann and Steve moved students into project-based groups that stayed together for the completion of a project. The attention to group skills in the flexible, temporary groups seemed to pay off since the project-based groups functioned well.

One project required students to present a formal argument concerning the United States' entry into World War II to two other teams. Steve and Lou Ann did not want the makeup of these groups to be left up to choice, so they carefully determined who would be in what group. They also determined group roles so that students would be interdependent. As previously stated, Steve and Lou Ann had, up to this point, randomly moved students into groups and assigned tasks without clarifying and modeling roles. This had not worked well. In fact, students, when given the choice of working alone or working collaboratively, frequently opted to work alone. For this project, however, Lou Ann and Steve were very intentional about making sure that the roles were linked to the tasks themselves:

- *Two Researchers:* Use two different texts to discover the facts about the United States' entry into World War II.

- *One Rubric Creator:* Construct a rubric with elements concerning "what are reasonable causes to enter a war." The rubric creator drafts the rubric for assessment. Then the rubric creators from each group meet, using their drafts to determine the class rubric.

- *Video Reviewer:* Record information about our entry into World War II based on video documentary.

▶ Checking In One More Time

"The final Friday of the school year was the best day of the year," Steve explained. "You should have seen them work."

No teacher familiar with the high school scene would have predicted Steve's heartfelt comment. Typically, by this time of the year, students have closed up shop and mentally begun their summer vacation, even as they sit at their school desks. So what happened?

The Friday before the last week of school, Steve and Lou Ann collected the commentaries and read through them over the weekend, but it took most of the following week to read them again carefully and then strategize on next steps.

They were very disappointed in their students' commentaries. Despite the models they had offered and the in-class conferences, the writing was generally boring and ineffective. Lou Ann and Steve suspected that students could do better, so on that last Friday of the school year, they cut a deal with their students.

Two grades were still needed for the grade book: the commentaries and a common assessment developed by the social studies department. The common assessment was optional, but Lou Ann and Steve had always had their students participate. This time, though, they used it as a bargaining tool. They told the students that they would substitute the commentary for their common assessment *if* students would put in the effort to improve their commentaries.

"Students eagerly sat down and wrote for the whole class period, even though it was the last Friday of the year," Steve enthusiastically noted. "This was a feeling of celebration. We caught them off guard with the rewrite, but by the end of the period, it was feeling celebratory, not punitive. First of all, four kids who hadn't turned the project in the first time came up and asked, 'Can I write mine?' and I said yes. Guess what their response was? They actually said, 'Sweet.' Nearly all of them turned in their papers the second time. For that whole class period, there was purposeful movement in the room. They knew they had to rewrite the entire paper, not just edit it. With twenty minutes left in the class, students were asking me if they could take it home and finish over the weekend. Can you imagine? So I made an announcement to the entire class saying that anyone who wanted to finish over the weekend was welcome to do so."

And the results? More than 93 percent of the students turned in their commentaries, and thirty-one of the forty-nine students earned either an A or a B. Remember, this was in a class where more than a third of the students were failing at the start of the unit. What a turnaround!

Making Time to Motivate and Engage

As we think back on our journey of coming to understand motivation and engagement, we are even more convinced that these two elements matter if we want students to become adults who think, who read, and who participate fully in our democracy. School is the place where many of us are initiated into what it means to be an educated person who cares about the world. It's the responsibility of schools to create the conditions that will catch our students' interest and motivate them to learn, and it's the responsibility of teachers to nurture engagement that gets students caught up in learning.

We can do this. We must do this.

Appendix: Science Times Seven

Planning Worksheet

Complete this worksheet by _____ and be prepared to share it with your teacher during the planning meeting. This worksheet does not necessarily contain your final decisions—it's still a work in progress!

Names:_____

Presentation Date: _____

PROPOSED TOPIC:

_____

_____

THREE FOCUS POINTS

Focus points can be subtopics that you would like to emphasize, science concepts that audience members should understand, or skills for the audience members to learn. Keep your focus points **narrow** so you don't try to tackle way too much in one presentation.

1) _____

2) _____

3) _____

Brainstorm! Write down your ideas for each section of the presentation.

SECTION 1: INFORMATION (5 MINUTES)

• How would you like to present the information? (poster, song, skit, poem, etc.)

_____

_____

• Which of the multiple intelligences will you engage and how?

_____

_____

• What are the most important things the audience must understand about your topic?

_____

_____

(continues)

Section 2: Activity (10–15 minutes)

• What are some activities that will help the audience learn about your topic?

_____

_____

_____

• How will you make sure that all audience members get to participate?

_____

_____

_____

• What materials will you need to gather for the activity?

_____

_____

_____

Section 3: Discussion (10 minutes)

• What is a real-world application of your topic?

_____

_____

_____

• What would you like the audience members to learn from the discussion?

_____

_____

Quiz (5-10 minutes)

• What are some pieces of information or skills that you can put in the quiz?

_____

_____

_____

(continues)

Name   **Responsibilities**

_____   _____

_____   _____

_____   _____

We held the planning meeting on _____

Teacher Signature: _____

Comments: _____

_____

Plan of Action

Our goals for block day include: Specifically what we accomplished:

_____   _____

_____   _____

_____   Teacher Signature:

                                      _____

Our goals include: Specifically what we accomplished by:

_____   _____

_____   _____

_____   Teacher Signature:

                                        _____

Our goals include: Specifically what we accomplished by:

_____   _____

_____   _____

_____   Teacher Signature:

                                        _____

Grading

Your final project grade will be 20% of your overall grade in Honors Chemistry and it will be based on rubrics for each section of the presentation. In order to earn high scores on the rubrics you must meet or exceed all requirements for each portion of the presentation and you must demonstrate an exceptional understanding of your topic. Remember that expectations are very high.

INFORMATION (16 POINTS)

Rubric Category	Score	Out of
Poster Design/Skit or Song Performance/Poem Reading (where it applies)		4
Mechanics/Writing		4
Length		4
Content		4

ACTIVITY (20 POINTS)

Rubric Category	Score	Out of
Relevance		4
Materials		4
Time		4
Audience Participation		4
Does it require thinking?		4

DISCUSSION (16 POINTS)

Rubric Category	Score	Out of
Article		4
Relevance		4
Time		4
Discussion Questions		4

QUIZ (16 POINTS)

Rubric Category	Score	Out of
Number and Type of Questions		4
Content		4
Level of Questioning		4
Reporting of Scores		4

(continues)

RESEARCH (32 POINTS)

Rubric Category	Score	Out of
Resources		4
Citations		4
Works Cited Page		4
Research Notes (completion)		20

DAILY QUIZ SCORES (90 POINTS)

1	2	3	4	5	6	7	8	9

PARTICIPATION IN DISCUSSIONS (10 POINTS)

Thoughtful Comments

TOTAL (200 POINTS)

Info	Activity	Discussion	Quiz	Research

Daily Qs	Participation	TOTAL	Out of
			200

(continues)

Section 1: Information Rubrics (Choose One)

Poster Rubric

Category	1	2	3	4	Score
Poster Design	Poster is sloppy and in pencil or pen. Handwritten and difficult to read. Not much effort is put into this product.	Poster is plain and/or not colored, with small type that is difficult to read. Students put minimal effort into this product.	Poster is organized and attractive with only a few design errors. The poster reflects student thought and effort.	Poster is creative, colorful, typed in a large font, and organized. Student made a strong effort to create a quality product.	
Mechanics	Poster has unclear or run-on sentences with more than 10 spelling and/or grammar errors.	Poster has some unclear language with 6–9 spelling and/or grammar errors.	Poster contains understandable language and only 3–5 spelling and/or grammar errors.	Poster is written in a clear and concise manner with 2 or fewer spelling and/or grammar errors.	
Length	The explanation of the poster takes 2 minutes or less.	The explanation of the poster takes 2–3 minutes.	The explanation of the poster takes 3–4 minutes.	The explanation of the poster takes at least 4–5 minutes.	
Content	Poster addresses few aspects of the topic, showing a very limited understanding of the concepts. Examples and diagrams are absent or inaccurate.	Poster addresses only some aspects of the topic as proposed in the planning meeting. Use of examples or diagrams is minimal, showing only surface knowledge of concepts.	Poster addresses all or most aspects of the topic as proposed in the planning meeting. It shows the concept through examples and/or steps, but it doesn't show in-depth comprehension.	Poster addresses all aspects of the topic as proposed in the planning meeting. It thoroughly demonstrates the concept through examples, diagrams, and/or steps.	

(continues)

Song or Rap Rubric

Category	1	2	3	4	Score
Performance	The performance of the song seems unpracticed and rushed. It's hard to understand the lyrics. Students perform with little energy.	Students perform the song without much energy or clarity. Some aspects of the song are interesting, but the performance shows minimal effort.	Students make few errors and perform with enthusiasm. The performance is organized, showing that students practiced the song.	Students perform the song with energy and commitment, making the meaning of the song clear. The performance was well-practiced.	
Writing	The song was written in a rush with lyrics that show little effort or creativity.	The lyrics are unoriginal and/or confusing.	The lyrics are well-written and clear to the audience.	The lyrics are original, interesting, and clear. The writing shows a strong effort.	
Length	The song doesn't have very many lines. Singing and teaching the song takes 2 minutes or less.	The song has fewer than 4 verses or very short verses. Singing and teaching the song takes 2–3 minutes.	The song has 4 verses and a chorus, with short lines. Singing and teaching the song takes 3–4 minutes.	The song has at least 4 solid verses and a chorus. Singing and teaching the song takes at least 4–5 minutes.	
Content	Song addresses few aspects of the topic, showing a very limited understanding of the concepts. Examples absent or inaccurate.	Song addresses only some aspects of the topic as proposed in the planning meeting. Use of examples is minimal, showing only surface knowledge of concepts.	Song addresses all or most aspects of the topic as proposed in the planning meeting. It shows the concept through examples and/or steps, but it doesn't show in-depth comprehension.	Song addresses all aspects of the topic as proposed in the planning meeting. It thoroughly demonstrates the concept through examples and/or steps.	

(continues)

Skit Rubric

Category	1	2	3	4	Score
Performance	Students read lines with their heads down, using minimal inflection and energy. There is no movement or interaction among the actors.	Students deliver their lines without much energy or clarity. Some aspects of the skit are interesting, but the performance shows minimal effort.	Students deliver their lines with little difficulty, making the meaning clear to the audience. The skit is fairly interesting to the audience due to the energy and effort of the performers.	Students perform the skit with energy and commitment. They are able to look up from notes and deliver lines clearly. Their creativity keeps the attention of the audience.	
Writing	The skit was written in a rush, with lines that show little effort or creativity.	The lines are unoriginal and/or confusing.	The skit is well-written and the lines are clear to the audience.	The writing is creative, interesting, and clear.	
Length	The skit takes 2 minutes or less.	The skit takes 2–3 minutes.	The skit takes 3–4 minutes.	The skit takes at least 4–5 minutes.	
Content	Skit addresses few aspects of the topic, showing a very limited understanding of the concepts. Examples are absent or inaccurate.	Skit addresses only some aspects of the topic as proposed in the planning meeting. Use of examples or diagrams is minimal, showing only surface knowledge of concepts.	Skit addresses all or most aspects of the topic as proposed in the planning meeting. It shows the concept through examples and/or steps, but it doesn't show in-depth comprehension.	Skit addresses all aspects of the topic as proposed in the planning meeting. It thoroughly demonstrates the concept through examples, diagrams, and/or steps.	

(continues)

Poem Rubric

Category	1	2	3	4	Score
Reading	The reading of the poem seems unpracticed and rushed. It's hard to understand the words. Students read with little energy.	Students read the poem without much energy or clarity. Some aspects of the poem are interesting, but the reading shows minimal effort.	Students make few errors and read with enthusiasm. The reading holds the attention of the audience.	Students read the poem with energy and commitment, making the meaning of the poem clear. The reading was well-practiced.	
Writing	The poem was written in a rush with lines that show little effort or creativity.	The lines of the poem are unoriginal and/or confusing.	The poem is well-written and the lines are clear to the audience.	The writing is creative, interesting, and clear.	
Length	The poem has very few lines. Reading and explaining the poem takes 2 minutes or less.	The poem has fewer than 5 stanzas or short stanzas. Reading and explaining the poem takes 2–3 minutes.	The poem has five stanzas with short lines. Reading and explaining the poem takes 3–4 minutes.	The poem has at least five solid stanzas. Reading and explaining the poem takes at least 4–5 minutes.	
Content	Poem addresses few aspects of the topic, showing a very limited understanding of the concepts. Examples are absent or inaccurate.	Poem addresses only some aspects of the topic as proposed in the planning meeting. Use of examples is minimal, showing only surface knowledge of concepts.	Poem addresses all or most aspects of the topic as proposed in the planning meeting. It shows the concept through examples and/or steps, but it doesn't show in-depth comprehension.	Poem addresses all aspects of the topic as proposed in the planning meeting. It thoroughly demonstrates the concept through examples and/or steps.	

(continues)

Category	1	2	3	4	Score
Relevance	The activity is not related to the topic.	The activity is somewhat related to the topic but students do not make the connection clear to audience members.	The activity is related to the topic. Students briefly discuss the connection between the activity and the topic.	The activity is highly relevant to the topic. Students show audience members the strong connection between the two.	
Materials	Students do not provide materials for the activity.	Students provide some materials for the activity. Some materials are disorganized or late.	Students provide all materials. They are prepared for most groups.	Students have all materials for the activity. They supply enough for all audience members.	
Time	The activity and explanation take 4 minutes or less.	The activity and explanation take 4–7 minutes.	The activity and explanation take 7–10 minutes.	The activity and explanation take 10–15 minutes.	
Audience Participation	The activity doesn't have any hands-on components.	Students only provide a pencil-and-paper activity.	Students provide a hands-on activity, but they don't get the audience members fully involved.	Students provide an engaging hands-on activity that requires audience members to work together.	
Does it require thinking?	The activity does not require much thought from the audience members.	The activity requires audience members to discuss the topic but it does not call for any analysis of ideas.	The activity requires audience members to think about a new situation related to the topic. It may not provoke in-depth analysis.	The activity requires audience members to analyze new information and develop a better understanding of the topic.	

(continues)

Discussion Rubric

Category	1	2	3	4	Score
Article	Students do not provide copies of the article for audience members. The article is very short and the source is questionable or it is not listed.	Students provide a very short article. They do not record the source of the article, or it is from a questionable source. They may not have enough copies.	Students provide each audience member with a copy of an article. The article may be too short or students might not show that it is from a credible source.	Students provide each audience member with a copy of a one-page article from a newspaper, magazine, or credible website. The article has at least 500 words.	
Relevance	The article is not related to the topic.	The article is somewhat related to the topic.	The article is related to the topic but it does not show how the topic applies to science or everyday life.	The article is highly relevant to the topic. It clearly demonstrates a real-world application of the students' topic.	
Time	Discussion of the article takes 4 minutes or less.	Discussion of the article takes 4–6 minutes.	Discussion of the article takes 6–8 minutes.	Discussion of the article takes 8–10 minutes.	
Discussion Questions	Students provide fewer than 5 question for discussion of the article and none of them are open-ended questions.	Students provide fewer than 5 questions for discussion of the article or all 5 questions are fact-based or closed questions.	Students provide 5 questions but some are fact-based or closed questions.	Students provide 5 open-ended questions to facilitate discussion of the article.	

(continues)

Research Rubric

Category	1	2	3	4	Score
Resources	Students listed three or fewer resources that supported their work.	Students listed only four resources that supported their work or five resources without hardcopy or database sources.	Students listed five resources, but they did not have both two hardcopy sources and one database source.	Students listed five credible resources, two of which were hardcopy sources and one of which was a database article.	
Citations	Students did not include any citations in the hardcopy of the information section (poster, skit, etc.).	Students included at least one proper citation in the hardcopy of the information section (poster, skit, etc.). Some information from outside sources was not cited.	Students included at least two proper citations in the hardcopy of the information section (poster, skit, etc.). Some information from outside sources was not cited.	Students included at least three proper citations in the hardcopy of the information section (poster, skit, etc.). All information from outside sources was cited.	
Works Cited Page	Students did not follow the MLA guide and wrote a disorganized works cited page.	Students partially followed the MLA guide for a works cited page (4–6 errors).	Students followed the MLA guide for a works cited page with 3 or fewer errors.	Students followed the MLA guide for a works cited page with no errors.	

(continues)

Quiz Rubric

Category	1	2	3	4	Score
Number and Type of Questions	The quiz includes fewer than five questions and questions are unclear or they are not written in the correct form.	The quiz includes only 5–9 questions and questions are unclear or they are not written in the correct form.	The quiz includes only 7–9 questions or the quiz includes 10 questions but some are not written clearly or in the correct form.	The quiz includes at least 10 questions clearly written in multiple choice, matching, fill-in-the-blank, or short answer form.	
Content	Only some of the questions require knowledge that audience members learned during the presentation. The quiz does not cover much of the content.	Most questions require knowledge or skills that audience members learned during the presentation. The quiz doesn't cover all aspects of the topic.	All questions require knowledge or skills that audience members learned during the presentation but the quiz doesn't cover all aspects of the topic.	All questions require knowledge or skills that audience members learned during the presentation. As a whole, the quiz represents a complete overview of the topic.	
Level and Quality of Questions	Questions are written to be simplistic and far too easy for the audience. They do not require much learning from the presentation. All questions are at the knowledge level.	Questions require knowledge from the presentation but they are very easy. There are fewer than three questions at the analysis or application level.	All questions require that audience members gained new knowledge and understanding of the topic. The questions are fairly easy or there are fewer than three questions at the analysis or application level.	All questions require that audience members gained new knowledge and understanding of the topic. The questions are reasonably challenging and at least three questions are at the analysis or application level.	
Reporting of Scores	Students grade only some of the quizzes or the scores are handed in after two days or in a disorganized format.	Students grade all quizzes but the scores are disorganized or they're not in a table. Scores are handed in within two days of the presentation.	Students grade all quizzes and report all scores in an organized table or spreadsheet within two days of the presentation.	Students grade all quizzes and report all scores in an organized table or spreadsheet within one day of the presentation (exam day presenters must report scores on the same day).	

May be copied for classroom use. © 2009 by John McDermott and Stevi Quate, from Clock Watchers (Heinemann: Portsmouth, NH).

Sample Quiz Questions
On the Topic of Acids and Bases

KNOWLEDGE QUESTIONS

Most of your quiz questions can be written at the knowledge level.

1. What is the Bronsted-Lowry definition of an acid?

   a) an acid creates H^+ ions in water
   b) an acid creates OH^- ions in water
   c) an acid is a proton donor
   d) an acid is a proton acceptor

ANALYSIS AND APPLICATION QUESTIONS

At least three of your quiz questions must be written at the analysis or application level. Analysis questions require students to analyze some information in the context of what they've learned.

2. A chemist tests a transparent solution with indicators. When she adds BTB to the solution it turns yellow and when she dips blue litmus paper in the solution, the paper turns red. This solution is probably:

   a) an acid
   b) a base
   c) a neutral
   d) an indicator

Application questions require students to apply some knowledge or skills to a new situation.

3. Write the balanced chemical equation for the neutralization reaction of potassium hydroxide and hydrobromic acid.

_____

_____

(continues)

MATCHING

Make sure the columns are organized.

4. Match the acid formula with the correct name.

     _____ HCl   a) hydrochloric acid

     _____ HNO_3 b) hydrosulfuric acid

     _____ H_2S c) nitric acid

     _____ H_2SO_4 d) sulfuric acid

FILL-IN-THE-BLANK

Make sure these questions are specific enough so there is only one possible answer.

5. When an acid reacts with a base, there are two products of the neutralization reaction. One of the products is _____ and the other product is a neutral ionic compound.

SHORT ANSWER

Make sure these questions are written clearly. Tell the student exactly what he or she needs to do.

6. Calculate the pH of a solution that has a hydrogen ion concentration of 0.035 M.

_____

_____

7. Explain why the pH will be greater than 7 when $NaC_2H_3O_2$ dissolves in a sample of water. Make sure you discuss the ions that are present in solution and any weak acids or bases that will form.

_____

_____

_____

Honors Chemistry Final Project

Names: _____

RESEARCH

20 facts are due at the end of the class period. Record your facts in the space below.

1. _____

2. _____

3. _____

4. _____

5. _____

6. _____

7. _____

8. _____

9. _____

10. _____

11. _____

12. _____

13. _____

14. _____

15. _____

16. _____

17. _____

18. _____

19. _____

20. _____

In the late 1990s Donald Graves (2001) set out to find the answer to a question: What gives teachers the energy to teach? About that same time, Sonia Nieto (2003) posed a similar question: What keeps teachers going in spite of everything? Both found that collaboration makes a difference for teachers and for students. Working with other adults energizes teachers, providing the fuel to keep going. This study guide is based on what Nieto, Graves, and countless other educators know: collaboration can create a vibrant learning environment that motivates educators and keeps them engaged in our profession.

Even though we know that many readers will read our book in a solitary manner, we hope that there will be others who will read with colleagues in order to explore our framework and its connection to their daily teaching lives. We hope that the conversation will be rich and stimulating and that the net effect will be seen in the classroom. The purpose of this study guide is to provide ideas for ways that the study group might progress and to offer thoughts about the role of facilitation.

The facilitator can either make or break the group. If there is no facilitator or if the facilitation is too laissez-fair, a group can go adrift and conversation devolve into the swapping of stories about the day and complaints about students. On the other hand, if the facilitator is too heavy handed, participants may avoid the difficult conversations that often emerge when teachers reflect on the challenges they face day in and day out.

It takes effective facilitation to keep the study group going in a productive manner. Our belief is that the facilitator's primary task is to keep the group motivated and engaged as they read this book. In order to do that, we offer the following tips.

Tip 1: Agreements matter.

Together, a groups needs to decide how they are will learn and grow together. Common issues, such as promptness, need to be tackled at the onset. The group needs to consider how airtime will be shared and what to do when someone dominates the discussion.

One way we've started this conversation is by presenting the group with a set of agreements as a starting point. What's important is that the group doesn't just adopt them without in-depth discussion. The group needs to wrestle with the implications of each agreement, determine if the wording is right for them, and figure out if the set is complete. It's important that the group arrive at their own consensus. Here are the agreements that we often begin with, but rarely does this initial set become the final set of agreements.

1. Be present. This agreement refers to the importance of each person being fully present on intellectual and emotional levels. For this to happen, even cell phones are silenced.

2. Be genuine and respectful. This agreement suggests that we will offer alternative viewpoints when our understanding differs from others. We agree that differences enrich our conversation, presenting insights we may not have considered.

3. Share the airspace. This agreement reminds us that all voices need to be heard and valued. Even though some people process their ideas verbally, this agreement reminds them that they cannot dominate the discussion.

4. Presume positive intention (Garmston and Wellman 1999). This agreement sets an important tone that encourages honest discussion and trust that all participants mean well.

5. Humor is welcome. Humor not only creates a caring atmosphere, but it enhances learning.

Tip 2: Ambiance counts.

Consider where you should meet. Is there an attractive and comfortable setting for the study group to gather? Is there a professional library or a conference room that would work well? Does a teacher live nearby who would be willing to open up her home for the study group? Consider the kind of mood that you want for an in-depth, reflective discussion. Staff developers at our former high school often planned study groups as if they were a High Tea. They would bring in sandwiches, special teas, and cookies. Diane Marino, a staff developer at our school, decorated the room with small twinkly lights from an old Christmas tree. Motivation and engagement applies to the teachers as well; *whatever you do, make this event a special time.*

Tip 3: Consider taking a broad view of perspective participants.

We often think of teachers as the participants of a study group; however, we encourage you to consider all who might be affected by motivation and engagement—or lack of it. Teachers care, but so do students, parents, paraprofessionals, counselors, and administrators. Consider how these various voices could enhance the discussion of the book. Some of our most energetic study groups have included teachers and students thinking together about educational issues.

Tip 4: A facilitator honors the learning of the group.

Facilitation means the act of making something easy, so a good facilitator makes the conversation of a group easy by keeping the conversation moving, honoring the agenda, and ensuring that all voices are heard. Notice that the facilitator is not an expert, rather a gentle leader who attends to the overall learning of the group. Consider whether or not one person will facilitate each meeting or if the role of facilitator changes each time.

Tip 5: Agendas—and routines—matter.

In the crazy, busy world of teaching, time is a huge issue. Teachers want to know that their time in any kind of professional learning situation is maximized. One of the many roles of the facilitator is to carefully plan each study group gathering. That, of course, means an agenda. But another way to think about this planning is to establish standard routines that participants can count on at each meeting. One routine that we've used is Connections, a short activity that starts each meeting. Since study groups often meet at the end of a teaching day, participants' minds are on the high and low points of the day. The routine of Connections provides a predictable bridge from the teaching day to the professional learning. It also is a routine that invites everyone's voice to join the conversation within the first few minutes. This activity provides a transition from the busyness of teaching into the reflective time of the study group. Typically 10 minutes long, Connections is an opportunity for people to mentally shift gears. The rules for Connections are quite simple:

1. This is a time to talk—or not to talk. If you chose to talk, you can tell a story about the previous evening, explain what's on your mind at this moment, or simply talk about your children's latest antics.

2. Don't speak unless you want to.

3. Listen to what others have to say, but do not respond. This is not a time for a conversation but a time to share—or not share—a thought about your thinking.

4. You may only speak once until everyone in the group has spoken.

5. Silence is fine. You might want to read for a bit, take a minute or two to jot down some thoughts in your journal, or reflect on your day.

6. Our agendas tend to reflect the routines that support us in doing good, collaborative thinking. Here is an agenda we've used often:

   - Connections

   - Follow up: Discussion of what participants tried with their students based on the last discussion.

   - Text-based discussion of the reading. (You might use generic structures, such as those listed on page 159, or specific questions, such as those in the discussion questions on page 160.)

   - Priming the pump: A short discussion or reflection that "primes the pump" for the upcoming reading so that participants think about the big ideas in the chapters ahead.

Tip 5: Determine what works best for the study group: open-ended protocols or text-based questions to guide the discussion.

In our discussion guide on page 160, we suggest questions for each of the chapters; however, the group may decide to use one of the following protocols to guide their discussion:

Save the Last Word for Me: Before the meeting, all participants select a section of the reading (e.g., a phrase, a paragraph, a sentence) that resonates with them. It may resonate because the reader loves the ideas, is confused by them, or disagrees with the text. At the meeting, divide the study group into small groups of four. One person in each group begins by reading the section that resonated for him but does *not* explain why. The rest of the members discuss the section while the first person listens to the discussion but does not participate in it. The goal of the discussion is to explore the ideas and the implications in the section, not to guess why it was selected. After about four to five minutes, the original participant stops the discussion and then gets the last word by explaining why he selected the quote. The conversation now turns to the next person, and the protocol continues until everyone has had an opportunity to have the last word about their selected section.

Final Word: Similar to the Save the Last Word for Me discussion protocol, each person selects a section that resonates for her prior to the meeting. However, the discussion follows a different process: the person reads her quote and explains why she selected it. Then in a "go around" each person in the small group has up to one minute to respond to the explanation either by adding ideas, presenting an alternate viewpoint, or making a new connection. The "go around" is done in round-robin fashion so that one person begins and the person sitting next to her follows. The original speaker has the final word after listening to everyone.

Four As: Prior to the discussion, everyone reads the chapter and answers each of the following questions of the four As. Of course, the answer is based on the ideas in the reading:

1. **Assume:** What do the writers assume to be true of you as readers?
2. **Agree:** What do you agree with?
3. **Argue:** What do you want to argue with?
3. **Aspire:** What do you aspire to?

The four As become the basis of the discussion.

Tip 6: Celebrate the learning of the group.

From the outset, decide how you're going to regularly celebrate the work of the group. Will this be done collaboratively or will you be solely responsible for planning the celebrations? How will you celebrate at the conclusion of the study group?

Discussion Questions for Each Chapter

The organization of our study guide is based on what we know about the reading process. Before we read, we need to activate background knowledge and set a purpose for the reading. We're calling that *priming the pump* and offer a series of questions intended to get participants ready for the reading.

For the questions specific to each chapter, we hope that the group will feel compelled to return to the text while they combine their own experiences with ours. For most of the chapters, we include an application question, some kind of a probe to urge teachers to take the ideas back to the classroom.

Before the group even begins the book, we encourage you to prime the pump with the following questions:

1. Prior to reading the book, talk about what you hope to gain by reading the book. What are your personal and collective goals?

2. When have you been a clock watcher? What were the conditions of the learning situation?

3. Reflect on a time when you learned something deeply. This learning could have occurred either in or out of school. For instance, you might recall the time you learned a complex algebraic formula that had baffled you or the time when you finally learned how to fly fish.

   a. Tell your story and listen to the story of others.
   b. Find commonalities: what characteristics did these stories share?
   c. Now reflect on a time when you were frustrated in a learning situation. Again, this could be in or out of school.
   d. Tell these stories, and find the commonalities.

▶ Chapter 1: Introduction

1. Explore the difference between holding and catching. Is the distinction important? Necessary?

2. Whose problem is motivation and engagement? The students? The teacher?

3. How did the notions of competency and control play into your stories about a time when you learned something deeply and a time when learning was frustrating?

▶ Chapter 2: Caring Classroom Community

Priming the pump for Chapter 2: Reflect on your favorite teachers when you were in school. What did those teachers do that made them special? How did they create a sense of community within their classroom?

1. Some teachers believe that taking time to do team building and other social activities is fluff. What do you think? How can building the caring classroom community contribute to learning? How could building classroom community detract from the learning process? The authors argue that building a caring classroom community is an ongoing process, not just a set of activities for the start of the year. Given your teaching situation, why might this be important and necessary?

2. What difference might it make if you were certain that not only do teachers know each other but students know each other well?

3. How will you incorporate the ideas in this chapter in your instruction even if you have a scripted or mandated curriculum? What will you commit to do before you meet again based on this discussion? How can your group collaborate to create caring classroom activities directly related to the curriculum?

▶ Chapter 3: Checking In, Checking Out

Priming the pump for Chapter 3: What are your beliefs about assessment? What role does assessment play in the learning process? In teaching? In grading?

1. What assumptions do the authors make about the connection among assessing, teaching, and learning?

2. How does checking in/out interplay with caring classroom community?

3. What can you do to bring students more into the assessment process?

4. How can you integrate assessment and grading?

▶ Chapter 4: Choice

Priming the pump for Chapter 4: React to this quote about choice:

> As common sense, as well as interest research, tells us, if students are doing the same activity day in and day out, boredom will inevitably set in. It is useful to have a variety of activities throughout the week, month, and school year. In addition, the introduction of novel ideas, content, tasks, and activities may facilitate situational interest. (Schunk, Pintrich, and Meece 2007)

Motivation theories suggest that providing some choice increases motivation. In this case, the focus is on building on individual's personal interest in a particular topic.

Although there is clearly a diversity of personal interests, many students share some interests. When teachers connect the lesson content to personal interests or common interests of the students, it can facilitate attention and situational interest.

1. What makes choice effective as a motivator/engager? Ineffective?

2. How does choice connect to checking in/out and caring classroom community?

3. How can offering choices improve student learning?

4. Look at something you are doing in the near future. With a partner, find entry points to add choice, such as choice of product, process, and content. Try it out and bring back the results. Do this even if you have a mandated or scripted curriculum.

▶ Chapter 5: Collaboration

Priming the pump for Chapter 5: What do you see as the advantages and pitfalls of collaboration? What have you tried that worked? That did not work?

1. Identify several common problems with collaboration among the study group. Review Chapter 5 to find ideas for addressing those problems.

2. Determine which of these levels of collaboration you tend to work in the most, and identify specific steps that you might try to move you up a notch. Use the chapter for ideas for those steps.

    a. Level X: Students almost never collaborate. Instead, discussion is directed toward the teacher or to the whole class.

b. Level 1: Short, focused opportunities for students to collaborate. The purpose is for students to work with a partner to address a singular goal, such as reflecting on an important point in the lesson or answering a question about the content. An example is pair/share when you ask students to turn to an elbow partner to discuss a specific topic.

c. Level 2: Collaboration at a deeper level that requires a variety of perspectives. Often collaboration at this level is also short-termed but requires more effort than collaboration at level 1. An example is moving students into triads to solve a problem or to synthesize ideas from several texts.

d. Level 3: Collaboration that requires students to work in groups for long-term projects or to collaborate over time. This includes students forming coaching teams to solve meaningful and challenging problems. Teacher modeling plays a critical role. Since these groups stay together for awhile, it's important for them to strategically choose group members, set norms, clarify roles, and assess their effectiveness as a group on a regular basis.

3. How does collaboration interweave with classroom community, checking in/checking out, and choice?

4. How will you incorporate the ideas in this chapter in your instruction even if you have a scripted or mandated curriculum? What will you commit to do before you meet again based on our discussion?

▶ *Chapter 6: Challenge*

Priming the pump for Chapter 6: Analyze an assignment that either did work well with a group of students or did not work well. Begin by determining the level of difficulty of the task: where on Bloom's taxonomy are you asking students to think (knowledge, understanding, application, analysis, synthesis, or evaluation)? What scaffolds do you have in place for the academically struggling? What do you have in place to challenge the academically motivated?

1. Respond to this statement: *All* students are motivated by challenge.

2. Discuss the connection between the appropriate level of challenge and the flow experience. When have you experienced this? How do you create the conditions in which flow is likely to occur in your classroom?

3. What's the connection between challenge and kids who are clock watchers?

4. Discuss the Schmoker quote: "Children in the earliest grades will argue with force and passion, will marshal evidence, and will employ subtlety on behalf of their favorite athletes, pop stars, and automobiles. This is the mind—the intellect—in action" (68). How can you bring this into the classroom into your next lesson/unit?

5. How does choice interweave with the other Cs in order to impact motivation and engagement?

6. How will you incorporate the ideas in this chapter in your instruction even if you have a scripted or mandated curriculum? What will you commit to do before you meet again based on our discussion?

▶ Chapter 7: Celebration

Priming the pump for Chapter 7: Is there time to celebrate students' successes in learning? Defend your position.

   If we were to create a culture of celebration within the school community, what difference would it make?

1. Effective celebrations begin with planning backwards. Why take the time to carefully plan for celebrations of learning?

2. How do celebrations enhance the six C framework?

3. Celebrations come in many forms; discuss the multiple approaches to celebrating learning.

4. For one class, track your celebrations and reflect on what difference those celebrations make for student motivation and engagement.

▶ Chapter 8: Putting It All Together

Priming the pump for Chapter 8: Is it realistic to incorporate all six Cs in an intentional manner throughout the year? What would you need to do to make this happen?

1. In triads, answer these questions:

   • If you were to take out one of the Cs which one would most impact motivation and engagement?
   • Now that you've the finished the book, how would you answer this question: So what?

2. As you read the methods employed by these teachers, what would you have done differently? The same?

3. How could your study group support each other as you try to implement the six Cs?

Works Cited

Garmson, R. J., and B. M. Wellman. 1999. *The Adaptive School: A Sourcebook for Developing Collaborative Groups*. Norwood, MA: Christopher-Gordon.

Graves, D. 2001. *The Energy to Teach*. Portsmouth NH: Heinemann.

Nieto, S. 2003. *What Keeps Teachers Going?* New York, NY: Teachers College Press.

Schunk, D. H., P. R. Pintrich, and J. L. Meece. 2007. *Motivation in Education: Theory, Research, and Applications*. Upper Saddle River, NJ: Prentice Hall.

WORKS CITED

Adler, M. 1982. *The Paideia Proposal: An Educational Manifesto*. New York: Collier Books.

———. 1983. *Paideia Problems and Possibilities*. New York: Collier Books.

———. 1984. *The Paideia Program: An Educational Syllabus*. New York: Collier Books.

Anderson, C. 2000. *How's It Going?* Portsmouth, NH: Heinemann.

Arvin, N. 2005. *Articles of War*. New York: Random House.

Bandura, A. 1997. *Self-Efficacy: The Exercise of Control*. New York: W. H. Freeman.

Beers, K. and B. Samuels. 1998. *Into Focus: Understanding and Creating Middle School Readers*. Norwood, MA: Christopher-Gordon.

Beers, K. 2003. *When Kids Can't Read: What Teachers Can Do*. Portsmouth, NH: Heinemann.

Begley, S. 2003a. "Expectations May Determine Outcomes More than We Realize." *Wall Street Journal*, November 7, B-1.

———. 2003b. "Real Self-Esteem Builds on Real Achievement Not Praise for Slackers." *Wall Street Journal*, April 18, B-1.

Brookhart, S. M. 2007–8. "Feedback That Fits." *Education Leadership* 65 (4): 54–59.

Brown, D. 2001. *Bury My Heart at Wounded Knee*. New York: Holt Paperbacks.

Csikszentmihalyi, M. 1990. *Flow: The Psychology of Optimal Experience*. New York: HarperCollins.

———. 1997. *Finding Flow: The Psychology of Engagement with Everyday Life*. New York: Basic Books.

Deci, E. 2006. "Student Motivation: What Works, What Doesn't." Transcript. Edweek.org Online Chat, August 30. www.edweek.org/chat/transcript_08_30_06.html.

Doyle, W. 1983. "Academic Work." *Review of Educational Research* (53): 159–99.

Dweck, C. S. 2006. *Mindset: The New Psychology of Success.* New York: Random House.

Education Week Press. 2006. "Student Motivation: What Works, What Doesn't." August 30. www.edweek.org/info/jobs.html.

Elias, M. J., M. C. Wang, R. P. Weissberg, J. E. Zins, and H. J. Walberg. 2002. "The Other Side of the Report Card: Student Success Depends on More than Test Scores." *American School Board Journal* 189 (11): 28–31.

Fay, J., and F. Cline. 1997. *Discipline with Love and Logic.* Golden, CO: Love and Logic Institute.

Fullan, M. 1993. *Change Forces: Probing the Depths of Educational Reform.* London: Falmer.

Gay, G. 2000. *Culturally Responsive Teaching: Theory, Research, and Practice.* New York: Teachers College Press.

Gewertz, C. 2006. "High School Dropouts Say Lack of Motivation Top Reason to Quit." *Education Week* 25 (26): 1, 14.

Goleman, D. 1995. *Emotional Intelligence: Why It Can Matter More than I.Q.* New York: Bantam Books.

Goodlad, J. 1984. *A Place Called School: Prospects for the Future.* New York: McGraw Hill.

Guthrie, J., and A. Wigfield. 1997. *Reading Engagement: Motivating Readers Through Integrated Instruction.* Newark, DE: International Reading Association.

Guthrie, J., A. Wigfield, and K. C. Perencevich. 2004. *Motivating Reading Comprehension: Concept-Oriented Instruction.* Mahwah, NJ: Lawrence Erlbaum.

Hidi, S., and J. Harackiewicz. 2000. "Motivating the Academically Unmotivated: A Critical Issue for the 21st Century." *Review of Educational Research* 70 (2): 151–79.

High School Survey of Student Engagement. 2005. Bloomington: Indiana University.

Holubec, E. J., D. W. Johnson, and R. T. Johnson. 1994. *The New Circles in the Classroom and School.* Alexandria, VA: Association for Supervision and Curriculum Development.

Johnson, D. W., and R. T. Johnson. 1998. *Learning Together and Alone: Cooperative, Competitive, and Individualistic Learning* (fifth edition ed.). Needham Heights, MA: Allyn & Bacon.

Johnson, D. W., R. T. Johnson, and C. Roseth. 2006. "Do Peer Relationships Affect Achievement?" *The Cooperative Link* 21 (1): 2–4.

Langer, J., with E. Close, J. Angelis, and P. Preller. 2000. *Guidelines for Teaching Middle and High School Students to Read and Write Well: Six Features of Effective Instruction.* Albany, NY: National Research Center on English Learning and Achievement.

LeCompte, M. D., and A. G. Dworkin. 1991. *Giving Up on School: Student Dropouts and Teacher Burnouts.* Newbury Park, CA: Corwin.

Marzano, R. 2001. *Classroom Instruction That Works.* Alexandria, VA: ASCD.

Melzer, J., and E. Hamman. 2004. *Meeting the Literacy Development Needs of Adolescent English Language Learners Through Content Area Learning.* Providence, RI: Brown University.

Moeller, V., and M. V. Moeller. 2002. *Socratic Seminars and Literature Circles for Middle and High School English.* Larchmont, NY: Eye on Education.

Myers, W. D. 2001. *Bad Boy.* New York: Harper Collins.

National Research Council. 2004. *Engaging Schools: Fostering High School Students' Motivation to Learn.* Washington, DC: National Academies Press.

NCREL. 2005. *Implementing the No Child Left Behind Act: Using Student Engagement to Improve Adolescent Literacy.* Naperville, IL: Learning Point Associates. www.ncrel.org/litweb/adolescent/qkey10/qkey10.pdf.

Neihart, M. 1999. Systematic Risk Taking. *Roeper Review.* 21 (4): 289–92.

Newmann, F. M., ed. 1992. *Student Engagement and Achievement in American Schools.* New York: Teachers College Press.

Peck, S. 1987. *The Different Drum: Community-Making and Peace.* New York: Touchstone.

Perencevich, K., and A. Taboada. 2007. "Classroom Practices That Nurture Reading Engagement." *Colorado Reading Council Journal* 18 (1): 5–16.

Ryan, R. M., and E. L. Deci. 2000. "Intrinsic and Extrinsic Motivations: Classic Definitions and New Directions." *Contemporary Educational Psychology* 25: 54–67.

Schmoker, M. 2006. *Results Now*. Alexandria, VA: ASCD.

Shernoff, D. J., M. Csikszentmihalyi, and B. Schneider. 2003. "Student Engagement in High School Classrooms from the Perspective of Flow Theory." *School Psychology Quarterly* 18 (2): 158–76.

Smith, F. 1987. *Joining the Literacy Club: Further Essays into Education*. Portsmouth, NH: Heinemann.

Smith, M. W., and J. D. Wilhelm. 2002. *"Reading Don't Fix No Chevys": Literacy in the Lives of Young Men*. Portsmouth, NH: Heinemann.

———. 2006. *Going with the Flow: How to Engage Boys (and Girls) in Their Literacy Learning*. Portsmouth, NH: Heinemann.

Sousa, D. 1999. *Brain Based Learning: The Video Program for How the Brain Learns*. Thousand Oaks, CA: Corwin.

Springs, M. A., and W. A. Kritsonis. 2008. "National Implications: Practical Ways for Improving Student Self-Concept Through Student Achievement." *Doctoral Forum: National Journal for Publishing and Mentoring Doctoral Student Research* 5 (1): 1–5.

Stiggins, R. 2001. *Student Involved Classroom Assessment*. Upper Saddle River, NJ: Merrill Prentice Hall.

———. 2005. "From Formative Assessment to Assessment *for* Learning: A Path to Success in Standards-Based Schools." *PDK* (December): 324–28.

———. 2007. "Assessment Through the Students' Eyes." *Educational Leadership* 64 (3): 22–26.

Tharp, R. G., and R. Gallimore. 1993. *Rousing Minds to Life: Teaching, Learning, and Schooling in Social Context*. Cambridge: Cambridge University Press.

Tomlinson, C. A. 1999. *The Differentiated Classroom: Responding to the Needs of All Students*. Alexandria, VA: ASCD.

Vygotsky, L. S. 1989. *Thought and Language*. Cambridge, MA: MIT Press.

Wentzel, K. R. 2002. "The Contribution of Social Goal Setting to Children's School Adjustment." In *Development of Achievement Motivation*, edited by A. Wigfield and J. Eccles, 221–46. St. Louis, MO: AcademicPress.

Wheatley, M. 2002. "Willing to Be Disturbed." In *Turning to One Another: Simple Conversations to Restore Hope to the Future*. San Francisco: Berrett-Koehler.

Wiggins, G. 2006. *Edutopia* (April/May): 49.

Wiggins, G., and T. McTighe. 2005. *Understanding by Design*. Alexandria, VA: ASCD.

Wiliam, D. 2007–8. "Changing Classroom Practice." *Education Leadership* 65 (4): 36–42.

INDEX

AbuSaeed, Shereen, 107–10, 115
achievement gap, 5
activity rubric, 148
Adler, M., 85
advanced classes, 16, 93, 95–96
After-School Seminars, 67, 69–70
agendas, for groups, 157–58
agreements, in groups, 155–56
ambiance, for group meetings, 156–57
American Studies Program (ASP), 69, 119–20, 124
analysis questions, 152, 131–32
Anderson, C., 46
application questions, 152
appreciation, job satisfaction and, 108
argument, structuring curriculum around, 101–2
Armour, Shaun, ii, 90, 124
Articles of War (Arvin), 69
Arvin, N., 69
assessment. *See also* checking in; checking out; grading; post-assessments; pre-assessments
    assessing practices, 48
    checking in and checking out, 8
    confidence building and, 34–36
    cynicism about, 32
    engagement and motivation and, 30–31, 33–34, 34–36
    feedback and, 38
    formative, 32
    forms of, 31–33
    gotcha factor in, 33, 38–39, 48
    grading vs., 33
    as high-stakes testing, 32
    involving students in, 37, 42
    options for, 136
    planning, 36–38
    student failure and, 33
    student folders for, 129–30

assignments
    choice in, 19, 20, 67
    learning styles and, 61–62
    music and, 63
    open-ended, 96
auctions, as mini-celebrations, 118–19
authentic accomplishment, 110
authentic research, 51
autonomy, 8
awards ceremonies, 121

Bad Boy (Myers), 45
Bandura, A., 34
bar graphs, for pretest charts, 35–36, 44
Basic Skills class, 121
Beers, Kylene, 2, 92
Begley, Sharon, 112
birthday celebrations, 113
bodily-kinesthetic intelligence, 20, 54
book celebrations, 120–21
boredom
    in advanced classes, 95–96
    challenge and, 101
Brave New World (Huxley), 50
Bridges, Olivia, 24
Brookhart, S. M., 45, 46
Brothers, Matt, 92–94
Brown, Dee, 68
Bury My Heart at Wounded Knee (Brown), 61, 68

Calder, Cindy, 60, 66
Card Passing, 128
caring classroom community, 8. *See also* classroom community
Carousel Brainstorm, 93
Cather, Willa, 2
Celebration Checklist, 115, 116

Celebration of Learning, 121–22
celebrations, 107–22
    discussion questions, 164
    engagement and motivation and, 9, 109–10
    every day, 113 114
    as fun, 110
    of group learning, 159–60
    of mediocrity, 110
    post-assessment and, 44
    pre-assessment and, 43–44
    preparing for, 107–8
    public, 109, 114
    teacher stance and, 111–15
    types of, 115–22
    value of, 108–10, 130–31
Center for Critical Thinking, 106
Center for English Learning and Achievement (CELA), 75
challenge, 95–106
    argument and, 101–2
    boredom and, 101
    classroom community and, 16–17
    discussion questions, 163–64
    engagement and motivation and, 9, 33–34, 96–98, 131–32
    flow and, 95, 97–98
    high, 97
    resources on, 106
    role of, 97
    simulations and, 102–3
    student skill levels and, 97
challenge project, 19, 21, 22
checking in, 8
    being intentional about, 47
    common assessments, 136
    discussion questions, 161
    feedback techniques, 44–47
    functions of, 32–33
    as process and product, 43

checking in, *continued*
  revision and, 47
  scaffolding and, 105
  student folders for, 129–30
  using teacher notebooks, 46
  ways of, 47
checking out, 8, 33
  discussion questions, 161
  as process and product, 43
  scaffolding and, 105
  student folders for, 129–30
children's books, student-written,
    121
choice, 49–71
  amount of, 55
  beyond the classroom, 67–70,
    132–33
  classroom management and, 50
  of content, 53
  discussion questions, 162
  engagement and motivation
    and, 8, 50
  frontloading and, 55–56
  in group work, 90
  honoring multiple intelligences
    with, 19, 20
  increasing options for, 70–71
  learning and, 53–55
  learning goals and, 51, 53
  meaningful, 53
  multiple intelligences and,
    53–55
  in process, 53
  in product, 52–53, 55
  purposeful, 51–52
  risks of, 70
  student achievement and, 63
Choices assignment, 57–60
class goals, 43
class poetry book, 108
classroom community. *See also*
    community of learners
  building, 14–16
  caring, 8, 12–28
  challenge and, 16–17
  collaborative, 91–92
  community-building activities,
    17–18, 125–29
  as community of learners, 16
  discussion questions, 161

emotions and, 13–14
fear of failure and, 17
importance of, 27
literacy club and, 16
unsupportive, 12–13
warm demanders and, 17
classroom culture
  changing, 11
  collaboration and, 91–92
  competency and, 11
classroom management, 50
class strengths, 43
Cline, Foster, 50
coaching groups, 77, 79–82
  auctions for, 118–19
  collaboration agreements, 80–81
  heterogeneous, 80, 81
  long-term, 133–34
  project-based, 135
  selecting membership for,
    79–81
coaching partners, 79
collaboration, 72–94. *See also*
    groups; group work
  challenging work for, 86
  classroom community and,
    91–92
  classroom culture and, 91–92
  difficulties of, 82, 85
  discussion questions, 162–63
  effectiveness of, 85, 90, 91
  engagement and motivation
    and, 8–9, 76, 85
  long-term coaching groups,
    133–34
  pacing, 86–87, 88
  project-based coaching groups,
    135
  resources on, 94
  role of, 8–9
  rubrics and, 89–90
  scaffolding and, 105
  in Science Times Seven, 83
  short-term flexible, 134–35
  teachers and, 138
  types of, 133–34
  value of, 76
  ways of working together, 79
collaboration agreements, for
    coaching groups, 80–81

Colorado Department of Educa-
    tion, 112
Colorado Writing Project, 114–15
common assessments, 136
community of learners, 16. *See
    also* classroom community
  celebration and, 110
  community-building activities,
    17–18
  creating throughout year,
    17–18
competency
  flow and, 11
  respecting student need for,
    10–11
conferences
  checking in through, 45–46
  student-parent, 113
Connections, 157–58
constructive criticism, 111
content, choice of, 53
content knowledge, 14
control, student need for, 10–11
Cooperative Learning Center,
    University of Minnesota, 94
creative learners, 59
Critical Friends Group (CFG),
    117
Critical Thinking Community, 106
Csikszentmihalyi, Mihaly, 2, 11,
    12, 13, 34, 37, 49, 50, 76, 95,
    97, 98, 104
curiosity, nurturing, 9–10
curiosity charts, 10

dancing, 122
Deci, E. L., 6, 45, 110
deep learning, 6
deficits, focusing on, 112
Delaware, University of, Problem
    Based Learning, 106
devil's advocate approach, 100
Dewey, J., 2
Discipline with Love and Logic
    (Fay and Cline), 50
discussion rubric, 149
discussions
  of political issues, 99–102,
    104–5
  protocols for, 158–59

diversity, celebrating, 119–20
Doyle, W., 19
dropout rates, 6
Dweck, C. S., 33
Dworkin, A., 7

economic level, motivation and engagement and, 6
Education of Little Tree, The (Carter), 61
Elias, M. J., 14
emotional intelligence, 19
Emotional Intelligence (Goleman), 14
emotions, learning and, 13–14
engagement
    assessment and, 30–31, 33–34, 34–36
    celebration and, 109–10
    challenge and, 33–34, 96–98, 131–32
    choice and, 8, 50
    collaboration and, 8–9, 76, 85
    economic level and, 6
    in high school, 6
    importance of, 2–3, 6, 136–37
    nurturing, 9–10
    parents and, 3
    self-confidence and, 39
    self-efficacy and, 34, 110
    in Science Times Seven, 66
    six Cs and, *xiii–xiv*, 7
    standardized testing and, 5–7
errors
    grading and, 114–15
    strengths *vs.,* 111–15
essential questions, 130
excellent work, modeling for students, 43
exit cards, 47
exit notes, 114
expectations
    high, 104–5
    learning and, 18–19
    low, 96
    power of, 112
    rubric descriptions of, 43
    scaffolding and, 104–5
    student perceptions of, 105

experiential learners, 57, 59, 61–62
external motivators, 42

facilitators, for groups, 157
failure, fear of, 17
Fay, Jim, 50
feedback
    importance of, 38
    techniques, 44–47
field trips, 50
fill-in-the-blank questions, 153
Final Word, 159
Finding Flow: The Psychology of Engagement with Everyday Life (Csikszentmihalyi), 12, 49
Fisher, Annie, 14–15, 28, 77
Fisher, D., 48
five-paragraph essays, 132
flexibility, in planning, 43
flexible groups, 77–79, 134–35
    coaching partners, 79
    4-2-1 activity and, 78
    skill levels and, 77
flow
    challenge and, 95, 97–98
    growth and discovery and, 98
    importance of, 2–3
    self-efficacy and, 34
    sense of competency and, 11
Flow: The Psychology of Optimal Experience (Csikszentmihalyi), 95
focus points, 139
formative assessment, 32, 37
4-2-1 activity, 78
Four A's, 159
Four Heads Are Better Than One, 88–89, 128–29
freewriting, 45
Frey, N., 48
frontloading
    choice and, 55–56
    ideas for, 56
    working together on, 79
Fullan, M., 11
fun, as intrinsic motivation, 110
Gallimore, R., 98

Gandhi, Mahatma, 30, 31, 33
Gardner, Howard, 19, 24, 53, 60, 63
Garmston, R., 156
Gay, Geneva, 8, 14, 15, 17, 104
Gewertz, C., 6, 8
gifted students
    coaching groups and, 80
    flexible groups and, 77
Gilbert, Judy, 112
Going with the Flow (Smith and Wilhelm), 10
Goleman, Daniel, 13, 14, 19, 38–39
Goodlad, John, 7, 8
gotcha factor, 33, 38–39, 48
grading
    assessment *vs.,* 33
    errors and, 114–15
    group work, 89–90
    learning *vs.,* 18, 27
    Science Times Seven, 142–43
Grapes of Wrath, The (Steinbeck), 60, 61
graphic organizers, 104, 130
Graves, Donald, 155
Gray, Katie, 53, 57, 63
Great Books and Great Ideas course, 16, 112
Great Gatsby, The (Fitzgerald), 61
groups. *See also* coaching groups; collaboration; flexible groups
    agreements in, 155–56
    ambiance for, 156–57
    celebrating learning of, 159–60
    coaching, 77, 79–82
    deadlines for, 134
    effective, 74–75
    facilitators, 157
    flexible, 77–79, 134–35
    heterogeneous, 37, 80, 81
    long-term, 133–32
    member selection, 74
    misunderstandings in, 91–92
    monitoring, 82–83
    participants, 157
    recorder's notes, 38
    role assignments in, 37, 93, 135
    role-playing, 74

groups, *continued*
  short-term, 134–35
  social loafing and, 82–83
  students as monitors of, 83
  teachers as monitors of,
    82–83
  teaching group skills, 74
  types of, 77–82
group work. *See also* collaboration
  accountability in, 87–89
  challenges of, 82, 85
  choice in, 73
  components of, 90
  designing, 85–87
  disinterest in, 72–73
  Four Heads Are Better Than
    One Quiz, 88–89
  grading, 89–90
  increasing student interest in,
    73
  independent work *vs.*, 76
  pacing, 86–87
  pair-share, 88
  panels, 87–88
  rubrics for, 83, 89–90
  Star Seminars, 85–86
  student monitoring of, 83–84
  teacher monitoring of, 82–83
Gulley, Marne, 107–8, 113–14,
    115
Guthrie, John, 6, 10, 55, 76

Hamman, E., 6
Harackiewicz, J., 2
Hartman, Karen, 113, 120–21,
    122
Heritage Day, 119–20
heterogeneous groups, 37
  process for building, 81
  value of, 80
Hidi, S., 2
high school
  celebrations in, 114
  engagement in, 6
  motivation in, 2
*High School Survey of Student
    Engagement,* 6
high-stakes testing, 32
Hiroshima unit, 55–56
homework, 66–67

Honors Chemistry Final Project,
    Research Day form, 154
Horizon High School, 68, 117,
    119, 132–33
humor
  Four Heads Are Better Than
    One, 88–89, 128–29
  learning and, 24

immigration project, 49–51
  choices for final projects, 51–52
  field trips for, 50
  finding people to interview, 50
  learning goals for, 51
incentives, pre- and post-assess-
    ments as, 42
independent work, 76
individual interest, 9–10
inquiry projects, 55–56
interest
  individual, 9–10
  situational, 9–10
internal motivators, pre-assessments
    as, 42
interpersonal intelligence, 20
intrapersonal intelligence, 20, 54
intrinsic motivation, 110
Iraqi War, 131–32

job satisfaction, 108
Johnny Got His Gun, 66
Johnson, D. W., 76, 80, 82, 90
Johnson, R. T., 76, 80, 82, 90
journals
  checking in, 47
  responding to student entries,
    26
  using, 26–27
  value of, 26

Kaehny, Sheila, 122
Kagan Publishing and Professional
    Development, 94
knowledge questions, 152
Kritsonis, W. A., 110
Kurtz, Kara, 34–35

Langer, J., 75, 76
Larner, Marjorie, *ix*
Lash, Steve, *x*, 124–36

learning
  emotions and, 13–14
  engagement and, 2–3
  expectations and, 18–19
  in the flow, 2–3
  formative assessment and, 32
  grades *vs.*, 18, 27
  humor and, 26
  motivation and, 1–3
  passion for, 49–51
  risk-taking and, 19, 21
  strategies, 45, 46
  threats and punishment and, 4
learning disabilities, 101
learning goals
  choice and, 51, 53
  multiple intelligences and, 63
learning preferences survey, 57–60
learning styles, 61–62
learning targets, 37
LeCompte, M. D., 7
linguistic intelligence, 20, 54
literacy club, 16
literacy histories, 15
literary coaching, 111
logical learners, 59
logical-mathematical intelligence,
    54

Magic Box, 26
Marino, Diane, 139
Martha's Café, 115
Marzano, R., 66
matching questions, 153
mathematical-logical intelligence,
    20
mathematics assignments, 67
McDermott, John, *ix, xiii,* 3–4, 7,
    12–13, 16–28, 33, 39–40, 48,
    57, 60, 66, 67–68, 76–79,
    86–87, 97–98, 115, 117,
    118–19, 121
McFarland, Martha, 115
McTighe, T., 37
mediocrity, 110
Meece, J. L., 162
Melzer, J., 6
memoir unit, 53
mentor texts, 39–40, 43, 132
mind maps, 21, 23, 24, 25

modeling
  excellent work, 43
  scaffolding with, 104
  zone of proximal development
    and, 98–99
Moeller, M. V., 85
Moeller, V., 85
monitoring
  groups, 82–83
  rubrics for, 83–84
  students and, 83–84
  teachers and, 82–83
Montbello High School, Denver,
  24, 114
Mosqueda, Marisela, 24
motivation
  assessment and, 30–31, 33–34,
    34–36
  celebration and, 109–10
  challenge and, 33–34, 96–98,
    131–32
  choice and, 8, 50
  collaboration and, 8–9, 76
  economic level and, 6
  in high school, 2
  importance of, 6
  individual interest and, 9–10
  intrinsic, 110
  lack of, 1–2
  nurturing, 9–10, 136–37
  parents and, 3
  post-assessment tests and,
    35–36
  pre-assessment tests and,
    35–36
  research on, 2
  situational interest and, 9–10
  six Cs and, *xiii–xiv*, 7
  standardized testing and, 5–7
  student perception of success
    and, 97
Moyers, Bill, 7
multigenre papers, 40
multiple intelligences, 24, 60
  assignments and, 19, 20
  choice and, 19, 20, 53–55
  homework and, 66–67
  honoring, 19, 66–67
  Science Times Seven and, 63
  types of, 54

music
  rubric for, 145
  signaling with, 128
  unit assignments and, 63
musical intelligence, 20, 54
Myers, Walter Dean, 45

National Research Council, 2, 6,
  13, 18, 50, 97, 99, 105
National School Reform Faculty,
  127*n*
Native Americans unit, 68–69
NCREL, 6
Neihart, M., 21, 22
Nelson, Lou Ann, *x*, 124–36
Newman, Pam, 55–56
Newmann, F. M., 110
Nieto, Sonia, 155
9/11, 131–32
No Child Left Behind, 5
notebooks, teacher, 46

observing, working together on, 79
open-ended assignments, 96
open-ended protocols, 158–59

Paal, Mandy, 31
Pacheco, Karen, 16–28
pacing, in group work, 86–87, 88
pair-share, 88
panels, 87–88
parents, sharing celebration with,
  113, 115, 117, 131
Paseo, 127–28
passion for learning, 49–51
Peck, S., 92
Perencevich, K. C., 6, 10, 55, 76
Peters, Thomas J., 109
photo-essays, 63
Pintrich, P. R., 145
Pitts, Leonard, 132
planning
  assessments, 36–38
  flexibility in, 43
poetry
  math assignments and, 67
  rubric for, 147
poetry slam, 107–8, 110
political convention simulation,
  99–102, 104

political issues, 99–102, 104–5
post-assessments
  as bookends for units, 40–41
  celebration and, 44
  charts, 35–36
  as incentives, 42
  learning targets and, 37
  matching with pre-assessments,
    42
  motivation and, 35–36, 38–39
posters, rubric for, 144
poverty
  motivation and engagement
    and, 6
  warm demanders and, 15
POWs (problems of the week),
  134–35
Pre-assessments
  as bookends for units, 40–41
  celebration of, 43–44
  excluding questions based on, 39
  as external motivator, 42
  graphs, 35–36, 44
  as incentives, 42
  as internal motivator, 42
  learning targets and, 37
  matching with post-assess-
    ments, 42
  motivation and, 35–36, 38–39
  student resistance to, 39
  when unnecessary, 39
prefixes, 78
pretest charts, 35–36
priming the pump, 160
problem solving, 79
Problem Solving unit, 60
process, choice in, 53
product, choice in, 52–53, 55
project-based coaching groups, 135
projects, choice in form of, 51–52
punishment, 4
purposeful choice, 51–52
Pyle, Ernie, 132

Quate, Stevi, *ix, xiii,* 1–3, 7, 9–10,
  14–15, 30–31, 33, 36, 38,
  39–40, 47, 48, 50, 51, 53, 55,
  56, 67–68, 76–77, 80–82, 83,
  86, 96, 98, 103, 109, 115,
  117, 122, 123

questions
    allowing time for answers, 103
    analysis of, 131–32
    for chapter discussions, 160–65
    in conferences, 46
    essential, 130
    for quizzes, 152–53
    role of, 103–4
    teaching students to ask,
        103–4
    text-based, 158–59
quizzes, 38
    for checking in, 47
    rubric for, 151
    sample questions, 152–53
    for Science Times Seven, 65

rap music, rubric for, 72
reading buddies, 121
reciprocal teaching, 93
recorder's notes, 38
Red Pony (Steinbeck), 50
research
    authentic, 51
    Honors Chemistry Final Project,
        Research Day form, 154
    rubric for, 150
    for Science Times Seven, 65
Research (Anderson), 46
researchers, in coaching groups,
    135
resource teachers, 104
Results Now (Schmoker), 102
reviewing a prior lessons, 79
revision, checking in through, 47
risk-taking, 19, 21
rituals, 109, 110
Roblin, Mike, 113
Rodriquez, Andrea, 72–76, 79
role assignments, in groups, 37,
    93, 135
role playing, 74
roll call, 14–15
Roseth, C., 76, 80
routines, for groups, 157–58
Rube Goldberg projects,
    121–22
rubric creators, in coaching
    groups, 135

rubrics
    for activities, 148
    cowritten with students, 42
    for discussions, 149
    for essential questions, 130
    for group work, 89–90
    learning preferences and, 57
    mind map, 25
    for poetry, 147
    for posters, 144
    for quizzes, 151
    for research, 150
    Science Times Seven, 142–51
    for skits, 146
    for songs and rap, 145
    student-friendly language for,
        37, 42
    student use of, 40
Ryan, R. M., 45, 110

Sages Grid, 57, 60–63
Santiago Baca, Jimmy, 7
sarcasm, 26
Save the Last Word for Me, 159
scaffolding
    activities, 104
    high expectations and, 104–5
    importance of, 106
    tips for, 105
    zone of proximal development
        and, 98–99
"Scarlet Ibis, The," 88
Schanke, Nancy, 34–38
Schmoker, Mike, 102
Schneider, B., 13
Schunk, D. H., 162
science activities, 64–65
self-confidence
    assessment and, 34–36
    engagement and, 39
    nurturing, in conferences, 45–46
self-efficacy
    engagement and, 34, 110
    flow and, 34
    task avoidance and, 76
self-esteem, 110
Science Times Seven, 57, 63–66
    collaboration in, 66
    elements of, 64–65

engagement in, 66
    grading, 142–43
    planning worksheet, 139–41
    rubrics, 142–51
Shernoff, D. J., 13
short answer questions, 153
simulations
    political conventions, 99–102,
        104
    value of, 102
Singer, David, 39–40, 114
singing, 122
site professors, 4–5
situational interest, 9–10
six Cs, xiii, 7–9
    braiding together, 123–37,
        164–65
    elements of, 8–9
    interrelationships among,
        123–24
skill levels
    challenge and, 97
    flexible groups and, 77
skits, rubric for, 146
Smith, Frank, 16
Smith, M. W., 7, 8, 10, 11, 34, 55,
    99, 103
social learning, 76–77
social loafing, 82–83, 90
social support, 78
Socratic seminars, 85
songs, rubric for, 145
Sparks, Susan, ix
spatial intelligence, 20
special education students,
    99–102
Springs, M. A., 110
staff development courses, 35
standardized tests
    engagement and motivation
        and, 5–7
    teaching to, 5–6
Star Seminars, 85–86
state assessment tests, 15–16
Stiggins, R., 34, 37, 38, 42, 48
struggling learners, 17
struggling readers, 121
St. Titus Grade School, Aliquippa,
    Pennsylvania, 4

student folders, 129–30
student-parent conferences, 113
students
    celebrating achievements of,
        109–10, 130–31
    celebrating strengths of, 111–15
    choice and, 63
    getting to know, 14–15, 17–18
    getting to know each other,
        17–18, 19
    involving in rubric writing, 42
    lessons taught by, 68–69
    modeling excellent work of, 43
    monitoring by, 83–84
    seeing potential in, 112–13
student-student interactions, 126
student writing, 47, 107–8, 110
study guide, 155–65
    agendas, 157–58
    agreements, 155–56
    ambiance, 156–57
    celebrations, 159–60
    discussion, 158–59
    discussion questions, 160–65
    facilitators, 155, 157
    participants, 157
study units, pre- and post-
        assessments for, 40–41
success, perceptions of, 97
Success Analysis protocol, 117–18
summarizing, 79
Super Saturday, 67–69, 133
survival unit, 53

Taboado, A., 10
task avoidance, 76

teachers
    celebrating student strengths,
        111–15
    collaboration and, 86–87, 155
    getting to know students, 14–15,
        17–18
    knowledge about motivation and
        engagement needed by,
        7–8
    monitoring self, 27–28
    as monitors, 82–83
    notebooks, 46
    questions asked by, 103–4
    respect for students' compe-
        tency, 11
    staff development courses, 35
    as warm demanders, 8, 15–16,
        17
teaching
    reciprocal, 93
    by students, 68–69
Tea Party, 92–93
technological developments, 60
telephone calls, 115, 117, 131
test anxiety, 30, 31
tests, student written, 30
text-based questions, 158–59
text messaging, 76–78
Tharp, R. G., 98
Thornton High School, 113
threats, 4
Tomlinson, Carol Ann, 77, 80
Tovani, Cris, xiv
tracking
    demoralization of, 4
    flexible groups and, 77

Treasure Island (Stevenson), 50
Trios, 128

video reviewers, in coaching
        groups, 135
video taping, 122
visual-spatial learners, 54
Vygotsky, L., 98–99

warm demanders, 8, 104
    classroom community and, 17
    role of, 15–16
Wellman, B., 156
Wentzel, K. 105
Wheatley, Margaret, 70
Wigfield, Alan, 6, 10, 55, 76
Wiggins, G., 37
Wilhelm, J. D., 7, 8, 10, 11, 34,
        55, 99, 103, 110
William, D., 32
"Willing to Be Disturbed"
        (Wheatley), 70
Wilson, Atwan, 114
Wilson, Kathleen, x
work triads, 60
World War I unit, 66
World War II unit, 55–56, 69–70
writing mentors, 132
writing style, 39–40
writing topics, 45

zone of proximal development,
        98–99

Ideas for motivating and engaging boys in literacy learning

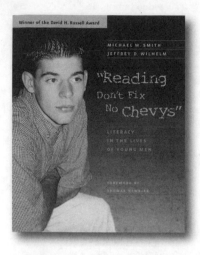

"Reading Don't Fix No Chevys"
LITERACY IN THE LIVES OF YOUNG MEN

Foreword by Thomas Newkirk

Michael W. Smith and Jeffrey D. Wilhelm's NCTE David H. Russell Research Award—winning book has helped tens of thousands of teachers connect with boys in secondary classrooms. This bestseller shares groundbreaking research on how boys can be motivated and engaged academically by bringing into the curriculum key aspects of the literacy lives they lead outside of school.

978-0-86709-509-8 / 248pp / $27.00

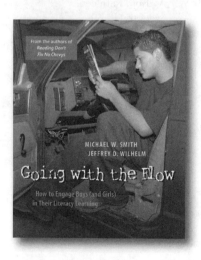

Going with the Flow
HOW TO ENGAGE BOYS (AND GIRLS) IN THEIR LITERACY LEARNING

Take *Chevys* out of the showroom and onto the road with classroom-tested units, lessons, and activities that get boys reading and writing and keep them involved in literacy learning. **Michael W. Smith and Jeffrey D. Wilhelm** fully illustrate their approach to designing and sequencing instruction—from developing activities that prepare students for success to fostering meaningful classroom discussions.

978-0-325-00643-7 / 192pp / $24.00

Sample Chapters available online at
www.heinemann.com

DEDICATED TO TEACHERS

TO ORDER CALL **800.225.5800** OR VISIT **www.heinemann.com**